ACTIVE
TUTORIAL WORK

Active
Tutorial Work

BOOK 3

Project Directors — JILL BALDWIN
HARRY WELLS — Programme Editors

BASIL BLACKWELL · PUBLISHER

ISBN 0 631 11741 5

Printed and bound in Great Britain
by Billing and Sons Limited and Worcester.

FOREWORD

Pastoral work in secondary schools has positive aims: the care of pupils as developing adolescents and the fostering of an efficient environment for learning. In the County's schools, "care" has long ceased to be synonymous with crisis counselling, and schools have exercised much thought in planning and developing education in human relationships as a positive part of their pastoral provision. The Active Tutorial Work books are a logical consequence of this growing interest and awareness, as is the significant, parallel programme of in-service courses and support group meetings which under-pin the whole of this work.

What "a school is" can be a potent influence upon a child's life, and can greatly affect the degree to which the school is successful in what it sets out to achieve through the curriculum. Active tutorial work, with its emphasis laid as much on approach as on content, can be a sensitising agent. It is concerned with feelings and with awareness, and may throw into sharp relief the pressures which surround the pupil in his daily life.

This carefully thought out series places the form teacher in his rightful place at the heart of pastoral work. I hope that it will be both stimulating and helpful to schools in their efforts to engage their pupils, actively, in their own personal growth and development, and I commend it to you.

A. J. Collier.
Chief Education Officer, Lancashire.

ACTIVE TUTORIAL WORK

This project was set up in response to the growing demand for worthwhile things to do in the form tutorial period. The aim has been to produce a coherent programme in which the approach is as fundamental and as important as the material.

A more direct approach to pastoral work began within the Lancashire authority in 1972 with the appointment of Ken David as specialist adviser for education in personal relationships. From this there developed a growing range of courses under the heading of Pastoral Care/E.P.R., concerned with enhancing skills such as counselling, interviewing and group dynamics and with broadening horizons. Within many schools the allocation of time for tutorials began to be increased slowly and some schools even allocated E.P.R. 'slots' on the time-table. There followed a phase when teachers, seeking for tutorial materials, adapted commercially produced resources from other areas of the curriculum, to this education for personal growth and development.

It became apparent, however, that there was a need to devise a teaching programme aimed at facilitating the pupil's personal growth and development through his own active participation.

In order to initiate such a programme a group of teachers was recruited, mainly from East Lancashire; they were invited to participate in an extensive practical course in developmental group work, so that programme writing could be started from a basis of common experience. A few of our teachers had previously been introduced to Developmental Group Work on courses run for the authority by Leslie Button of Swansea University, whose continued support and advice has been invaluable during the development of our project. When this training programme was completed, it was then possible to begin to devise a programme of tutorial work for five years of secondary education. This programme was to be essentially practical and based heavily on the developmental group work approach. There would be 'threads' running through all the years, for example, self-picture, self-respect, and the development of learning and study skills, as well as themes which the team deemed to be particularly applicable to specific years. In putting these ideas into practice the project team are grateful to Douglas Hamblin of Swansea University, another of our mainsprings of inspiration, for allowing us to adapt some of his materials.

It is important to emphasise that the resulting programme is not an ad hoc collection of materials; there has been a determined effort to create a rationale for the work, i.e. that it is developmental and has clear aims and objectives stated in small simple steps wherever possible so that teachers and pupils can observe for themselves that something is being achieved.

Training in the acquisition of certain key skills, and continued support for teachers who are attempting to train their colleagues in school, have been central parts of the project. This means that teachers have had not only access to materials, with accompanying guidelines, but also the opportunity to participate in in-service training focused on close work with young people. This has been aimed at developing social skills by meeting people, skills of listening and conversation, step-by-step discussion, coping with relationships with authority figures, with family and peer group relationships and with feelings about self and the ability to make friends.

It is 'teacher style' which makes even the most carefully documented programme unique in every classroom situation. It is mentioned here because it is of paramount importance when working in the field in inter-personal relationships to be aware of what we, as teachers, bring to the situation, that is to know ourselves, our mannerisms, our beliefs, attitudes, prejudices and the signals which we give. In short, we should be sure that our 'being' is in accord with what we are saying and what we are trying to do.

To sum up, this tutorial programme is not concerned with the administrative side of a teacher's pastoral role, nor with crisis counselling. It is concerned with assisting a young person with his own normal growth and development, with developing his social competence and with weathering the passing storms of growing up to become increasingly the master of his own destiny.

J. Baldwin and H. Wells
Project Directors

WRITING TEAM

Mrs. J. Baldwin
Curriculum Development
Officer, Blackburn

Mrs. S. Armour
St. George's High, Blackpool
Field Officer

Mr. H. Wells
Curriculum Development
Officer, Burnley

Mrs. M. E. Longstaff
Everton High, Blackburn

Mrs. S. B. Mealls
Hollins High, Accrington

Mr. C. Crewe
Walton High, Nelson

Miss A. R. Baldwin
Towneley High, Burnley

Mrs. S. Clay
St. Hilda's R.C. High,
Burnley

Mrs. K. M. Chambers
Towneley High, Burnley

Mr. A. Burrows
Hollins High, Accrington

Mr. A. Scholes
Barden High, Burnley

Mr. M. Thornber
St. John Fisher R.C. High,
Preston

Mr. T. Bryant
Skelmersdale College

Project Directors — Jill Baldwin Harry Wells — Programme Editors

CONTENTS and PLANNING GUIDE

LIST OF APPENDICES

TO THE TEACHER

Your initial reaction when reading through this programme may have been that there is far too much for one term or one year's work, particularly if your tutorial time is brief.

The programme pre-supposes a time allocation of an hour per week with the tutor group. Even so, there is a great deal to work through. The writers hope that you will try to tackle all the themes, for most of which a variety of approaches and strategies have been suggested, to allow for differing situations and your own preferences. We hope, however, that you will not choose only the 'safe' topics and approaches, but will branch out and tackle those which may be more demanding and problematical for you.

Another reaction may have been that some of the activities are too simple and 'childish'. Again, an attempt has been made to provide for all ability levels. However, we ask sincerely that activities be *tried* before being condemned as too simple or inappropriate for your particular group. You may be surprised by your group's responses.

The programme is not intended to be followed rigidly, step by step, week by week, although there is a rationale for the order in which the work is presented. After careful consideration, we felt that certain topics were essential in the first term, and some in the first half of that term. However, if a theme or topic presents itself naturally at a different stage in the year, we hope you will be able to find a course of action in the programme to fit your needs at the time.

Furthermore, the programme is certainly not intended to be a 'Definitive Guide to Tutorial Work'. We hope you will continue to use your own strategies and approaches where these have proved to be successful for a particular purpose. We would ask, however, that you keep 'one eye' on your objectives to ensure that all are being given equal status.

Finally, we don't expect miracles! A single session on many of the themes can, obviously, have only a limited effect. Therefore, we hope that you will be able to return to them, recapitulating and building on what has gone before. Above all, we hope that both you and your pupils will enjoy your 'Active Tutorial Work' together.

THE MAIN AIMS FOR TUTORIAL WORK IN THE THIRD YEAR

To recognise and meet the differing demands of upper school courses, project work and examinations.

To link the work of school with the world of work encouraging enquiry, thought and reflection, in order to broaden horizons on career and further education opportunities.

To facilitate further the acquisition of sound habits in planning and using private study time.

To put academic pressures, the use of leisure, and teenage feelings of boredom into perspective.

To encourage personal reviews of progress and to see parent/staff co-operation in a positive light.

To continue to develop:
  competence in social skills
  listening skills
  the ability to empathise with others
  the ability/willingness to participate in group endeavours
  the ability/skill to plan and conduct personal conversations.
and to use these to facilitate contact with and understanding of outside agencies.

To continue to develop flexibility and sensitivity in inter-personal relationships through deeper consideration of the processes of labelling, stereotyping and stand-point taking.

To encourage the further growth of a positive self-picture through self-assessment, reflection and moments of introspection.

To help pupils to understand their relationships with authority, and the norms and pressures which groups bring to bear upon their members.

To bring about an appreciation that there is a balance between greater freedom, which young people demand, and responsibility.

To examine the social/personal aspects of health hazards, such as smoking, alchohol, drugs.

To relate the facts of sexual development to personal feelings and responsible behaviour, and to examine the changes in relationships with the opposite sex.

To examine roles in the family and in relationships with friends and adults.

To look outwards, beyond self, friends and peers, to the consideration of making a positive contribution to the local community, and to an appreciative examination of major national and international issues.

ABOUT AIMS AND OBJECTIVES

It is useful for us, as teachers, to have a fairly wide range of objectives which are clearly and precisely expressed, in order to plan the learning opportunities for the pupils and to devise means of assessing the extent to which the pupils have achieved the stated objectives. It is fairly common to find a list of objectives carefully and precisely stated at the beginning of subject syllabuses, integrated projects and the like. These have been thought out in terms of pupil learnings and the type of responses which will demonstrate the learning, usually some form of examination or test.

Stating objectives is another matter, however, when it comes to 'affective' and 'emotional' learning, the values and attitudes which are part of the educational process.

We tend to speak in general terms when referring to the 'pastoral' side of education, and to use words and phrases rather loosely. This leads us to feel that there is general agreement about the purposes of education, that we all know what we are trying to do, so we do not need to spend time discussing it or writing it down. In fact, when terms are defined and discussion pursued, agreement is not so widespread.

The members of this project feel that it should be possible to state clear objectives for affective education, and put forward the following propositions:

(a) That the personal development of the pupils is equally important and should be as carefully planned and organised as their cognitive development.

(b) That a planned scheme for personal development will enhance and underpin all the cognitive learnings planned by the school.

(c) That objectives for personal development should state the type of behaviour to be observed so that, if it is observable, some attempt can be made to measure the change and, therefore, assess whether objectives are being achieved.
It should not be assumed that they are being achieved.

(d) The objectives should state what the *pupil* can achieve in observable behavioural terms. There will be different levels of achievement, as a member of the class group and as an individual, and the pupil himself should be central to the process of keeping the objectives under review.

(e) Objectives should be unambiguous, should communicate to others a clear intention, and give an indication of content. A simple but important criterion is: 'What will the pupil be doing?'

WORKING IN GROUPS

WHY HAVE GROUPS?

The project's approach to Tutorial group work is based on Leslie Button's expressed belief[1] that such work is 'about helping children in their growth and development, in their social skills, their personal resources and in the kind of relationships they establish with other people. Social skills can only be learnt in contact with other people;' . . . and it is the purpose of active tutorial work to provide each pupil with practical situations where he is in constant interaction with others, can try new approaches, experiment in new roles, develop insights, come to know and to help himself and seek to establish personal goals.

WHAT KIND OF GROUP?

To most teachers, group work usually suggests half-class groups or groups of ten to sixteen pupils. The usual reaction to this is that 'It's impossible to have half-classes or groups of a dozen in our school', and that group work is thus a non-starter in their situation.

Whilst some schools have managed to create a climate in which pastoral group sessions of 12-16 have become a norm, we believe that it would be unrealistic to plan a programme of active tutorial work, for each of the years eleven to sixteen, on the supposition that this would become the norm in all schools. Thus we have based our programme on the premise that the form teacher will be working with the whole classes, or large groups, which he will then break down into small groups — sometimes of three or four, sometimes five or six, sometimes based on the friendship patterns in the class and sometimes based on other criteria which are applicable to a particular situation or activity. These groups have something in common with the buzz group, embrace something of the discussion group, and are often particularly concerned with the exploration of feelings. What we seek is maximum participation and interaction for each pupil, even though we are faced with a whole class/large group situation, and therefore we require more than two, but preferably not more than five or six youngsters in our small groups if we are truly to achieve active tutorial work for all.

STEP-BY-STEP DISCUSSION

It is not difficult to stimulate discussion amongst a whole class group when it is broken down in this way, by posing a series of questions. After the question has been discussed in groups for a few minutes the teacher may call for the attention of the whole class/group so that they may report to one another interesting points which have arisen in their small groups. These exchanges usually lead quite naturally into the next question, which is then fed back to the small groups. This is referred to as step-by-step discussion. The important skill for the teacher lies in being able to foresee a series of questions, each of which represents a small step forward. The ability to foresee possible outcomes, and thus to arrange a programme of questions, has to be balanced by a genuine open-ness to change and to unforeseen responses if real dialogue is to ensue.

Many middle to lower ability pupils will be unable to discuss abstract concepts, (e.g. relationships) and one has to begin at the level of simple recall:

> 'Who were the first two people you met this morning?' (Groups then work at this together.)
>
> 'Who else did you meet?'
>
> 'Who did you think was the most important person you met?' (More small group discussion. Perhaps — What do we mean by important?)
>
> 'How did you behave towards each other?'
>
> 'Who spoke first?'
>
> 'How did you feel?' . . . etc.

Then, perhaps move on to a more general discussion on relationships, difficulties experienced in meeting other people, and so on.

The early stages of their discussion will last only a few minutes and are not meant to be exhaustive, but rather to open up discussion, stir ideas, encourage participation.

This type of group work is an effective way of involving and activating young people, leading them step-by-step into deeper understanding, accelerating exploration and involving everyone in active participation in new experience. It is not formalised, is easy to initiate, and seems to have the effect of allowing the individual pupil to formulate tentative ideas and rehearse statements which he then feels better able to bring forward to the whole class — often with the support of his small group behind him.

The teacher's role is to encourage contributions from one group after another, to move in close to the groups from time to time, to intervene, to suggest points missed, add emphasis, crystallise, support and draw out the timid and the soft-spoken, and yet demonstrate that he is including everyone in the general exchanges. His sense of pace is important — more often moving things forward in a lively way, yet allowing pauses for introspection or a greater depth of contemplation. He must also be sensitive to feelings and be able to convey warmth and encouragement.

[1] L. Button: *Developmental Group Work in the Secondary School Pastoral Programme*, page 1, Department of Education, University College of Swansea, June 1978.
[2] This technique has been developed by Leslie Button and described by him as 'Socratic Group Discussion' in L. Button: *Discovery and Experience*, pp. 120-126, O.U.P., 1971 and L. Button: *Developmental Group Work with Adolescents*, pp. 151-161, Hodder & Stoughton, 1974.

USING VISITORS [1]

Although this technique is introduced initially as a social technique in the 1st year, we have put it to wider use in succeeding programmes because our experience has proved it to be an invaluable tool for learning. Whatever the reason for inviting a visitor to school, the youngsters take so much more from the session when they are actively involved in conducting it than when they are the passive recipients of a prepared talk.

Although we have provided agendas within the first and second year programmes to try to take teacher and class along together, stage by stage, we feel that it is important to give a fuller account here. As the teaching programme progresses, ways in which the visitor technique can be usefully employed often arise naturally out of the work. In the first place, however, it usually arises from direct suggestions by the teacher. So let's start from there.

The question is put, *'Shall we have a visitor to the group?'* This is followed up by, *'Who shall it be?'* A short but lively session ensues with questions such as, . . . *'Who will invite the visitor? . . . How will it be done? . . . When will it be? . . . How long will it last?'* . . . are discussed, until the broad details are decided.

The next consideration is, *'What do we want to know, or find out, from our visitor?'* Ideas may flow freely or may have to be initiated by strong prompting from the teacher. You may wish to jot the random ideas down on the board, or the group might wish to appoint a scribe. Next, the group sifts through the ideas . . .

'Which can we use?'

'What might make the best opening question?'

'Who's going to ask the second question?' and so on, until the opening stages of the session are beginning to take shape. The group might then consider, *'Is there anything we specially want to tell the visitor?'* and after that, *'Will the visitor want to ask us any questions?'* *'Who's going to ask this?'* etc.

By now we're turning to, *'Who's going to greet the visitor?'* *'You, Suzy? How are you going to do it? Come on . . . show me.'* *'Right, now let's try it again . . . . is that O.K.?'* and so on. Then

xviii

might follow questions and short role plays about how the visitor will feel, how he will be put at ease and made to feel welcome, until everyone is quite sure about what will happen and what is to be said. This knowledge, this detail, this sureness engenders confidence and a sense of security.

Then, on again . . . . *'Where will the greeting take place? Will it be at the classroom door . . . at the school entrance? Come on, Suzy, show me — imagine I'm your visitor . . . Oh, by the way, what are you going to talk about as you walk through the school with the visitor?*
. . . Come on, the rest of you, help her . . .'
These are very active stages with lots of interruptions, questions and short snatches of role play . . . . *'Stop, show me! Good, now let's try again . . .'* etc.
'Now we've reached the room, are you going to introduce everyone?
You are? Go on, then . . . show me.
Where do we sit? How do you want the room arranged?
Come on then, let's do it like that.
Now, who's going to ask the first question? Right, fire away.'
and so on to the next and the next. Then, *'Fine, that's going nicely, so let's go back and start all over again. First, who's going to play the part of the visitor? Jack? Good . . . off you go to the main entrance. Ready, Suzy? Ready, everybody? Off we go again!'*
We work our way through the whole situation again stopping, prompting, questioning, involving the whole group in a corporate wish to do something well. You might find, additionally, that the group wishes to discuss and sort out the organisation of tea and biscuits.

Preparation of the visitor is as important as the preparation of the group. The visitor will need to know a little about the nature of the group and the work you're doing as well as about the situation and the kind of questions he can expect to meet. The visitor must anticipate a certain stiltedness about the first few questions and be briefed not to talk at length or to rush to fill in the small silences which might arise, in case he cuts across some of the questions which the youngsters have so carefully prepared. *Very important;* ask your visitor to be punctual — to the minute if possible. The group builds up to a point of keen anticipation and a late arrival can kill the spontaneity which will be present in the situation, despite its having been carefully rehearsed.

It is not unusual for teachers to 'put off' the first visitor session, saying 'My group isn't ready yet.' Don't delay; experience has shown this to be a most unifying experience and is often the point at which 'the group takes off!' Your hardest job, as a teacher, is to sit back, shut up and leave it all to the youngsters when your visitor arrives. One of your most rewarding moments comes when the youngsters gather round afterwards, bursting to talk about the experience, sharing a corporate sense of 'Didn't we do well?' and quite sure that they can do even better next time.

To summarise: Certain basic questions need to be considered in preparing for the occasion, and procedures need to be well-rehearsed so that everyone may feel confident about their own contribution, e.g.

* Who do we invite and for what purpose?
* What do we talk about?
* Who asks the questions? In what order?
* Can we make sure everyone says something, even the shy members? How do we help them to do this?
* How do we prevent certain members dominating the occasion?
* Can we ask personal questions? Dare we ask . . . about . . .?
* Where would be the best place to meet?
* Do we provide refreshments? If so, who looks after these?
* How do we greet the visitor on arrival? What do we say/do?
* Where should he sit when he arrives? What about us?
* Who will actually extend the invitation? Do we do this in writing or in person?

Abbreviated extracts from a report by practising colleagues.

In preparing a group for a visit, the teacher will be concerned that it should:

offer them the opportunity for practising their social and conversational skills, and developing these further;

prove useful to those who have difficulty in social exchanges with adults and strangers, especially any shy and withdrawn members;

be an opportunity for group members to support those who are in difficulties, and increase support generally in the group;

be a rewarding occasion for the visitor himself.

The *range of possible visitors is almost endless . . . other members of staff (including all ancillaries); pupils might even get to understand why the caretaker doesn't like it when things are put down the toilets!*

Parents: in terms of occupation, interests, or as parents. Medical personnel and public figures (e.g. police, careers, vicars . . .) Elected members of councils and trade union representatives. Official representatives of industry, public relations officers, etc.

Not all visitor occasions are successful, for a number of reasons, but often because of lack of preparation with the group or with the visitor. One or two members, or the visitor himself, may have dominated the situation. Some groups can be so overcome by their own self-consciousness that they are unable to carry through what they have practised. It is important that the first visitor to such a group is sensitive to their difficulties and can help to overcome them.

Surprisingly, experience has shown that it is often the young people who would seem to be the least likely to appear socially competent, who come forward as the most able in meetings with visitors, whilst the apparently more competent ones seem often to become tongue-tied and self-conscious. Young people have been surprised and delighted at carrying off the occasion. They gain significance in their own eyes through the willingness of an adult to speak freely with them, and are often eager for the next visit to take place. In this way, the contribution of the visitor to learning can be considerable.

[1] J. Jordan: *The Role and Contribution of the Visitor in Developmental Group Work*, Department of Education, University College of Swansea, 1977; and L. Button: *Developmental Group Work with Adolescents*, pp. 86, 110, 163, Hodder & Stoughton, 1974.

NOTES ABOUT ACTION RESEARCH

It is a fundamental principle of this tutorial programme that the pupils should become actively engaged in making their own discoveries about themselves and their relationships. A matter of outstanding importance is the degree to which the pupils are committed to, and engaged in their own learning. This work sets out to encourage this commitment by using a process which Leslie Button has called Action Research. Thus, if the pupils are actively engaged in finding out for themselves, what it is like either to be in someone else's shoes or to take on some responsibility on another's behalf, then their discoveries can have a strong impact on them and stir a determination to take some action about the situation which they have uncovered. Moreoover, through their enquiries the pupils will have already begun to affect the situation which they are examining.

Action research may be seen as a series of developing steps:

1) A line of enquiry which has stirred the group to want to take some action, is identified.
2) Some of the group may be 'commissioned' to carry out a pilot enquiry. For example, the topic may be anything from an enquiry into people's problems of getting to school, to an examination of loneliness arising out of a friendship study, or an enquiry into the world of work, or life in the sixth form.

3) The main enquiry is then undertaken and it is important to guide the group in an examination of the possibility of their taking some action.

Objectives for action should be limited, as it is vital that the youngsters should feel that there is a possibility of bringing about some change in the situation under review. Similarly, the plan of action decided upon should be well within the time span that the pupils are likely to be able to sustain.

The value of Action Research lies in the central part played by the pupils themselves. They are involved from the beginning in diagnosing the problem, discussing (in small groups) different strategies for action, preparing enquiry forms and articulating the plan for themselves, with the help and guidance of the tutor.

Action Research is a valuable tool in helping to foster an individual's own growth and development, particularly where personal difficulties impede this growth. It is a way of helping a person to see beyond himself, so that he becomes not merely aware of the needs and problems of other people, but is moved to make a personal contribution.

References
Dr. L. Button: *Developmental Group Work with Adolescents*, Unibooks, Hodder & Stoughton, 1974.

NOTES ABOUT ROLE PLAY

The term 'role play' has been used fairly frequently in this programme and, in fact, is introduced to the group early in their experience together. After initial laughter and silliness to cover embarrassment, the pupils normally respond and enjoy the physical action which seems to relax the situation and bring discussion to life. By acting out how they think someone would behave in a situation, they can be encouraged to consider what it is like to be in someone else's shoes.

Role play should arise spontaneously in response to a need to communicate 'what it was really like' or 'might have been like'.

Therefore, it may arise out of discussion or contribute to it, and may help less secure youngsters in the group to 'rehearse' whatever is the next little step forward for them. It may help, for example, to prepare for meeting strangers, carrying out conversations and meeting people in authority. It will help them to become used to the idea of the new experience before the actual event and to have confidence in their own participation.

Role play is not seen as something special, a 'big production', for which a specialist is needed, but as an essential part of active tutorial work, flowing in and out of the events as they occur, e.g. 'Don't tell us − show us.'

NOTES ABOUT STUDY SKILLS[1]

A frequent complaint with pupils, as with students, is 'I can't get started' or 'I worked all night and I still know nothing', or 'I can never remember anything' . . . and so on.

The study skills section extends 'care' to caring about a pupil's progress and his ability to work and study efficiently. In bringing this concern into the area of Pastoral Care and active tutorial work, there is no deep laid plot to usurp the functions of the English department or interfere with the requirements or philosophies of other subject areas. In this programme we suggest approaches to teachers in various departments for co-operation and assistance; it could be that these approaches may lead to a re-appraisal of differing subject demands.

The Third Year work does not stand alone and should be seen as a continuation and development of the work which was begun in the first and second years. It is hoped that teachers will refer back to and build upon this previous work.

As with all the other sections of this book, the Study Skills section is seen as being *active* tutorial work with the teacher fully involved in a continuous dialogue with individuals, with the different groups, and, at times, with the whole form.

[1] See also Hamblin: *The Teacher and Pastoral Care*, Chapter 3, Basil Blackwell, 1978.

DEEPENING ROLE PLAY

We have employed simple role play in several parts of our first and second year programmes in order to practise or look more closely at the parts which are played by members of the class in various situations. There are times when we feel the need to deepen the explorations of individual or group relationships with other people, in a way which will add impetus to the investigation and depth to the supportive nature of the group. Thus, *socio-drama* is designed to involve the whole group in creative thinking and feeling, and in willingness to help: it is also concerned with the real-life situations which surround them. In operation it may have the spontaneity of simple role play, but is a little more organised in that the teacher may 'cut' any phase of the role play at any time in order to ask questions, highlight incidents, or move the action on to look at the same "characters" in other company and in other situations.

The teacher will determine the tempo of the work in his 'cutting', and in the vigour with which he leads the group to (a) examine the feelings which are brought into the open, and (b) identify with (get into the skins of) the characters involved in the role play.

In practice he may choose to role-play an incident from the pupils' experience: stop it — ask 'onlookers' how they saw it: 'cut' again, and follow the same characters to another situation to see if their behaviour changes. He may well stop the action to ask if the 'actors' really feel like, or share in the feelings of, the people they are portraying.

He may ask: 'Was it really like that?' and will often lead the participants to 'try that again' (using his sensitivity and judgement of timing so as not to break the continuity) or may ask: 'What happens next?' 'How did you react?' . . . etc.

Many people may be involved as the action moves from one setting to another, or in contributing to the running discussion; everyone can feel involved and personally touched by such an (unscripted) investigation of situations of social concern.

Socio-drama can be changed subtly into the form known as the *Social Documentary*. This is still basically role play, but involves a mixture of planning and spontaneity and uses the audience to further the action.

As the role play is now to be 'presented to an audience' there must be some planning and discussion about the situation to be presented, how it should move, and the kind of situations/incidents to be highlighted, but the expression of thoughts, feelings, actions and reactions is left to the 'players' and is completely spontaneous.

The 'audience' is invited to assume the role of the significant people who surround the group, e.g. vandals may portray their acts of vandalism and need a response from the audience on the part of their victims, police, teachers, parents, court . . . when investigating adolescent relationships with adults, an audience of parents would form a ready-made group of significant adults in a teenager's life. The pupils may well direct the 'performance' themselves with, maybe, some assistance from the teacher in persuading parents to participate and become involved in the running discussion which will be going on. It is a sharp experience for both players and audience. The experience enables youngsters to look at themselves with great objectivity and if, like the parents in the situation we have used, the audience are people who are concerned for the youngsters involved, then some creative contacts and insights may have been made which may be the beginnings of an extended dialogue in the home and a new pattern of relationships.

For a fuller treatment see Dr L. Button: *Developmental Work with Adolescents*, pp. 92-96, Unibooks, Hodder & Stoughton, 1974.

NOTES ABOUT LISTENING

The development of listening skills is central to the personal growth of pupils taking part in the Active Tutorial Work programme, and the team would hope that teachers are constantly aware that, alongside the stated objectives for each activity or theme, other objectives are also being pursued.

The objectives, when we listen to people, are both basic and simple:

1 We want people to talk freely and frankly.

2 We want them to cover matters and problems that are important to them.

3 We want them to get greater insight and understanding of their own values and attitudes (problems) as they talk about them.

4 We want them to try to see a situation clearly from where they themselves stand.

In the course of this work, we hope to encourage children to be aware of themselves as listeners and to avoid:

1 hasty interruption or argument,

2 passing judgement too quickly, or in advance,

3 jumping to conclusions, or making assumptions on too little evidence,

4 allowing the speaker's sentiments to react too directly on their own.

In addition, we hope that the pupils will not allow their feelings about a person or a situation to colour their judgement.

These points are easy to understand intellectually, but the real problem is in applying them effectively in our relationships with other people. This requires practice, repetition and awareness.

PRACTICAL TRUST ACTIVITIES

These activities can be used to introduce the ideas of trust, concern and support which are difficult concepts to explain. Actually experiencing putting one's trust in a person or a group of people is much more meaningful than talking about trust at an abstract level. However, the activities for trust building require quiet, reassuring leadership. Teachers may find it valuable to try them with a group of their own colleagues before using them with children. This will increase confidence and allow the teacher to experience the activity for himself so that he understands the feelings which the children may experience. An alternative, or further, step would be to lead the activities in a smaller group, of twelve or fifteen, with whom the teacher has a comfortable relationship.

Teachers may feel that pupils, especially the older ones, will react adversely to this kind of activity by being noisy and silly. This does sometimes happen, of course, in which case it is important to stop the activity and discuss why they are reacting in this way. If the teacher is able to treat the topic of 'trust' seriously and naturally, without embarrassment, the pupils can be encouraged to try again, overcoming the awkwardness and embarrassment which they may feel. Quite often the pupils respond to the activity quite seriously, and will gain a great deal from it, and the subsequent discussion about their feelings will be serious and constructive.

EXAMPLES

Blind Trust

The pupils are asked to find a partner, one of whom will keep his eyes closed as a 'blind' person. His partner will lead him around the room, negotiating furniture and other people, and, if possible, continuing outside the room, where the 'blind' person becomes more disorientated and, therefore, more dependent. After about six or eight minutes, the partners are asked to change roles, so that each has a turn at leading and at being led.

The pupils are encouraged to hold their partners comfortably and securely and, at the same time, describe the textures, colours and shapes which are encountered. The leader, in this way, helps the 'blind' person to 'see' through his (the leader's) eyes.

The teacher will encourage thoughtfulness and a concern for helping the 'blind' person to feel safe. Discussoin afterwards would be about how far this was achieved, styles of leading, what happened when other people were encountered, and so forth.

Supporting in Pairs

In pairs, roughly of equal height and weight, one person stands with eyes closed, with his back to his partner. The other person places his hands comfortably on his partner's shoulders and supports the weight of his partner, who leans gently backwards. As this person relaxes, the partner has to support more weight and take care to make his partner feel 'safe'. Partners then change over, to experience both supporting and being supported.

Supporting in Threes

As above, but the person in the middle now has someone in front as well as behind, on whom to lean. This usually helps to make people relax more easily as they lose their fear of falling forwards. Each person should have a turn in the middle, whilst the teacher circulates, encouraging a relaxed feeling.

Supporting in Groups

A volunteer stands, with eyes closed, in the centre of a close ring of five or six people, who support the person in the centre, as he sways gently from one to another. A feeling of group concern for the person in the middle is generated, and silence and concentration should be encouraged. The group can then lift the person gently to shoulder or head height and sway him backwards and forwards before lowering him to the floor, or placing him back on his feet again. Others are then encouraged to take turns in the middle.

This is a real opportunity to *feel* what being cared for is like, if the activity has been led quietly and purposefully. It is important to focus on how easy or difficult it feels to place one's trust in the hands of others, as well as or how trustworthy one allows oneself to be when responsible for someone else.

These kinds of activities are not ends in themselves and should be repeated on different occasions to continue the process of building trust and a caring atmosphere within the tutor group. This atmosphere is especially important when dealing with aspects of relationships, such as friendship, family and feelings of self-worth.

If such an atmosphere is carefully nurtured, there will be a wonderful opportunity for members of the tutor group to help one other to grow and develop in self-esteem and personal responsibility.

Autumn Term

Pupil Objectives	Activities	Organisation and Method
To continue to show concern for others in the form and to give his support.	**RENEWING THE CONTRACT** *Shaking hands is not just a social convention; in our form it means we belong to this group, and we mean to contribute positively.*	**You will need:** Sheets of paper, pins, pencils, cassette player and tape. The teacher reminds the class of the previous years' activities for getting to know one another. People may have left, new ones come, so the pupils are asked to shake hands, say 'Hello' to everyone, making sure they meet new people or those whom they don't know very well. The teacher asks pupils to sit with someone other than a friend, and chat for a few minutes – the agenda opposite may help to get things moving.
To develop further the confidence to speak in the company of others, and to demonstrate sensitivity to other people's feelings.	**CONVERSATIONS** *Agenda* Did you have a good holiday? What did you enjoy most? Was there anything which you disliked? Why? What do you remember best about it? (Extend the above into a fuller agenda.) *An Appraisal of the Second Year* Examples of statements might be: 'I started to like P.E.' 'I couldn't do my maths, history, etc, homework.'	The pupils think of two statements about themselves and what they thought of the second year at school. These statements are then written, fairly large, on a piece of paper, and each pupil pins his own paper on his chest. They then walk around in silence, reading everyone else's statements. (Music in the background helps to break the ice.)

Pupil Objectives	Activities	Organisation and Method
To review his progress to date, realistically, both from his own point of view and from the point of view of others.		After several minutes, when the music stops, the teacher asks the pupils to go to the person whose statements interested them most, i.e. Who did you want to question or agree with?
		They may go to more than one person. After a few minutes the teacher asks everyone to sit down in twos and threes and talk about the report which they had at the end of the second year. The agenda opposite will help to focus attention.
	Agenda When I read my last report I felt . . . When my parents read my report, they said . . . . I was pleased with my report because . . . I was unhappy with my report because . . . . My attendance last year was . . . . My best subject was . . .	The pupils are encouraged to complete the statements verbally, one to another, and discuss what they have said. The teacher moves around, giving out the next statement quite rapidly.
To describe his expectations of life as a third-year pupil.	*Aims For The Third Year* This year I am going to do better in . . . I am looking forward to . . . day at school because . . . . I am not looking forward to . . . day at school because	The teacher continues in a similar manner, using statements which begin to focus on the year ahead.

AUTUMN TERM

Pupil Objectives	Activities	Organisation and Method
To know the new time-table and organisational changes.		**You will need:** Time-table blanks, paper
	WHAT'S NEW THIS YEAR?	Pupils look at their new time-tables and identify any changes, e.g. new rooms, subjects.
	1 Pupils fill in blank time-table with subjects and rooms only.	Pupils work in small groups. The teacher asks each group for the names of the teachers of each subject, listing these on the blackboard and adding names omitted, particularly of teachers who are new to the school.
	2 Pupils to list, for each subject, the teachers who may teach them during the third year:	The teacher asks the pupils to identify those teachers who will teach the form.
	Subject	Teacher		
	3 Pupils add teachers to the time-table.	
	4 Points to note: Are there any administrative changes, e.g. different dinner arrangements? Are there 'geographical' changes, e.g. parts of the school which the third-year pupils may or may not use?	
	5 A quick time-table 'test': e.g. Where will you be at 10.00 am on Wednesday? What is period 3 on Friday?	Follow-up after about one week. Identify all changes and any problems. This could be made into a competition if desired, along 'Bingo' lines, filling in spaces according to the answers.
		You will need: Another time-table blank

3

AUTUMN TERM

NOTE: It could be worthwhile to repeat this activity later in the year in order to find out whether the pupils still perceive both themselves and others in the same way. (Who has 'grown' and how?) Pupils will need to note the labels which they have ascribed to others and also the labels ascribed to them, for this future reference.

Pupil Objectives	Activities	Organisation and Method
To develop a greater awareness and acceptance of himself.	*WHO AM I?* The participants pin labels on each other's backs. By questioning the rest of the group they try to identify the name on their label.	**You will need:** Sheets of card/paper, 15 cm x 8 cm Pins Fine, felt-tipped pens — useful but not essential
To become able to assess himself accurately and understand other people's assessment of him.	The original version of this activity used labels based on people in the public eye, similar to those shown below: — Margaret Thatcher Terry Wogan Angela Rippon Harold Wilson Vanessa Redgrave Kevin Keegan Virginia Wade Magnus Pike These would be prepared by the teacher/course organiser before the session. From these labels laid out on a table, each participant would choose a label (name) which he felt suggested some characteristic(s) which might be appropriate to a particular member of the assembled group.	1 Lay out the paper, pins and pens before the session begins. 2 Explain the activity to the class. Each person is to try to think of someone they know locally (maybe in the class or the school) or, alternatively, someone from public life, who in some way shows physical, temperamental, emotional resemblance(s) to a member of the class. They then write the name upon which they have decided on one of the sheets of paper/card provided, in large, clear print. 3 From this point there are two alternative lines of procedure. a) Having written his label, the writer pins it on to the back of the member of the group/class for whom he thought it was appropriate. The recipient should NOT see the label. The disadvantage of this alternative is that more than one person will write a label for some pupils whilst no-one will have prepared a label for others.

4

Pupil Objectives	Activities	Organisation and Method
To develop a greater awareness and acceptance of himself. To become able to assess himself accurately and understand other people's assessment of him.	*WHO AM I?* (continued) This activity has been used successfully with both teachers and pupils. It is, however, often more successful with pupils when they choose the names on the labels for themselves and may include people whom they know personally, as suggested in the next column. (See 3 opposite.)	b) Tell the class that if they can think of appropriate names/labels for more than one member of the class they may do so if they wish (but limit this to two or three). Next, collect all of the labels together on a table and then ask the class to look at all these labels and choose one, other than the one(s) which they have written, and pin it (unseen) on to the back of a fellow-pupil for whom they think it appropriate. With more labels than pupils there is less chance of pupils 'missing out' in the labelling process. 4 The pupils then begin to move around the room, asking questions of the rest of the group in order to identify themselves, 'Am I well known?' 'Am I a man?' 'Do people like me?' 'Am I local?' 'Would I like myself?' 'Am I serious/funny/a sportsman?' The pupils may ask no more than three questions of any one person at one time, before moving on to ask and answer questions with another member of the group.
To be involved in his own personal growth through an examination of his self picture, feelings of self-esteem and the way others see him.	*Agenda for discussion* (See 5 opposite.) Were you surprised/pleased/put out by the label given to you? Why? What surprised you most? What have you learnt about yourself?	Participants cannot ask anyone 'Who am I?', but when they think they have guessed the identity of the person on their label they may ask someone, 'Am I . . .?' If they guess wrongly, they continue asking questions, as before. If they guess the correct identity, they still stay in the 'game' to answer questions from others about their labels. 5 The activity is followed up by class discussion. See the Agenda opposite.

Pupil Objectives	Activities.	Organisation and Method
To be involved in his own personal growth through an examination of his self-picture, feelings of self-esteem and the way others see him.	*WHO AM I?* (continued) The teacher could ask who wrote certain labels and why. If alternative (b) was used, did someone else give this label to someone else other than the person for whom the writer intended it? Why? Does this mean we all see people differently? These labels perhaps describe only one facet of a person. Therefore, can we choose a label for each person in the group which would be kind or reassuring? Examine reasons for these choices. How do the recipients feel? Which labels would they choose for themselves? Why? Ask, can others see 'you' in this role or see these qualities in you? *Agenda for discussion* If you wanted to be different (to change your label), could it be done? Is it easy or difficult? What would others in the group have to do in order to let you change? Would they have to behave differently towards you? Do you need this sort of help from people or can you change all by yourself?	
To show concern and provide support for his peers when statements about difficulties or anxieties are heard.		

Pupil Objectives	Activities	Organisation and Method
To be able to assess himself accurately; to understand the assessments made of him, by others; to make choices of subjects and levels that reflect his abilities and aspirations most appropriately. To begin to assess the qualities and attainments which upper school work will demand. To review his progress to date realistically, both from his own point of view and from the point of view of others. To be able to examine attitudes, progress and achievement (e.g. giving up too easily, 'couldn't care less', going along with the rest).	*KNOW YOUR OWN SKILLS – A GUIDE TO DECISION MAKING* 1 What are your skills? Are you going to use the skills you have? What are the skills you need to develop?	You will need: APPENDIX 1a: *Know Your Own Skills* self assessment form. 1 Teacher distributes the self-assessment skill enquiry form. (APPENDIX 1a). The items listed on the form should be discussed in order to clarify the terms used. It may be necessary to take one section at a time, going on to the next section when the pupil has completed the previous one. 2 Pupils will then fill in Column 1 on the form, individually. During this time, the teacher is advised to observe what the children are writing, so that comments can be made to the pupil who may have a low self-opinion.

Pupil Objectives	Activities	Organisation and Method
To assess himself accurately; understand the others' assessment of him; make choices of subjects and levels that reflect his abilities and aspirations most appropriately.	*Agenda for discussion* Do others rate your skills differently? Have you been too confident? Have you underestimated your skills? Have you an accurate picture of your particular skills, strengths and weaknesses?	Each pupil should ask a partner who knows him well to complete the form again, using Column 2. Fold the page over or hide Column 1 so that the friend will not be influenced by what has been written in that column. Encourage the pupils to be honest with each other, by reminding them that they are trying to help each other to make important decisions. The pupils should keep the forms for future reference, so that Column 3 can be completed at a later date for comparison.
To be involved in his own personal growth, through an examination of his self-picture, feelings of self-esteem, and the way others see him.	Are you satisfied with your skill score? Is there anyone who can help you? Can you do things to help yourself?	The pupils will have copies of their assessment sheets. The pupil selects from the form: 1 examples of five skills which he does well; 2 examples of five skills which he considers satisfactory; 3 examples of five skills in which he needs help.
To demonstrate his ability to make the most effective use of time and mental energy by producing plans for study and revision.		Class or small group discussion to help one another to summarise the skills required in various subjects and to consider whether a particular subject would be a wise choice. A summary sheet is provided. --- **You will need:** APPENDIX 1b: *Know Your Own Skills*, paper, summary sheet, pens, pencils

8

Pupil Objectives	Activities	Organisation and Method
To be able to identify the influence which friends, peers, parents and teachers can have upon making choices.	*PEOPLE WHO INFLUENCE US* APPENDIX 2 gives a series of situations with a list of people who might bring some influence to bear on what a pupil does. After completion, does a pattern emerge? *Agenda for Discussion in Pairs* Who seems to have the most influence on you?	You will need: APPENDIX 2 *People Who Influence Us* APPENDIX 3 *Why Do I Listen?* Coloured pencils Give out copies of APPENDIX 2 to each pupil. Ask the pupils to complete the list, placing a tick under the person whose advice they should seek in each situation. This activity may be done individually, but comparisons can be made, in pairs, as the sheets are completed.
To be able to look at the part he and his fellows play in groups, and develop some awareness of the different parts which people play in different situations.	Does this change in relation to the importance of the decision to be made? Which are the really important decisions? Who helps you to make these? *Why do I Listen to Them?* APPENDIX 3 gives a list of people to whom we may turn for advice, and reasons why we would listen to them. *Agenda for Discussion* Who appears to be the most influential or important person? Why have some people on your list been left out? For what kinds of things do you turn to your friends?	*N.B.* The agenda should be used briskly to encourage thought about the activity, with a brief pause between each question to allow pupils to tell each other of their findings and their opinions. Distribute copies of APPENDIX 3. This is an individual exercise. Useful discussion will follow, by sharing the results with a partner or in small groups. Pupils complete the left-hand column, adding the names of any other persons, and then link each person, with a coloured arrow, to the most compelling reason for listening to advice.

AUTUMN TERM

NOTE: Some pupils can learn more effectively through visual stimulation. Similarly, some can express their thoughts, ideas and even feelings more easily and effectively by visual means.

This activity uses simple diagrams as a stimulus for discussions on self-perception and inter-personal relationships. It is a technique which, once begun, can be employed wherever and whenever it would facilitate the discussion of personal feelings and personal relationships.

It is important to rid the pupils of any sense of inadequacy in drawing by demonstrating that simple pin-men drawings will suffice.

Pupil Objectives	Activities	Organisation and Method
To examine relationships with others in a variety of situations, at home, at school, with friends or with adults.	*WHAT'S GOING ON HERE?* 1 '*This was me yesterday!*' Why are you waving your arms? Are you happy? Are you angry? Are you alone? (Here an addition may be made to the drawing.) Who are they? (The others in the drawing.) Is it because of them, or something which they've done or said, that you're waving your arms?	You will need: Paper and pencils 1 a) Draw a simple match-stick man on the blackboard (see example opposite) to represent yourself as you might have been (or might have felt) in a recent social situation and say to the class something like: 'This was me yesterday!' adding, after a pause: 'What do you think I was doing?' Then encourage the class to question you in order to find out more about the situation. Discussion might develop along the lines suggested opposite. Additions can be made to the drawing as and when questions make them appropriate. b) Once the class has grasped the idea and questions begin to flow easily, halt the proceedings and ask if one of the class would now like to draw himself on the blackboard in a situation of his choice. Encourage questions as before.
To develop a greater awareness and acceptance of himself.		

Pupil Objectives	Activities	Organisation and Method
To examine relationships with others in a variety of situations, at home, at school, with friends or with adults.	*WHAT'S GOING ON HERE?* (continued) *'This was me yesterday!'*	It is important that the pupils *see* this activity as an aid in exploring their own situation and not as 'snooping' or seeking gratuitous information.
	2　Pupils draw diagrams of life situations involving themselves. Start with simple situations: Yourself at breakfast time today. You with the first person you met today.	2　Pupils should now work in twos, taking turns to draw their diagrams and ask each other questions about them. After these two initial examples, each pair could share their diagrams and their discussions with another pair for a few moments.
To develop a greater awareness and acceptance of himself.	They could then follow up with situations such as: You and a policeman. You at play. You at work. You and a friend. You at home (with Mum/Dad). You and the rest of the class. Situations/areas of concern which may be important at the present moment. This can be extended to: a)　Draw yourself as you see yourself: *now* (fold the paper); in *10* years (fold the paper); in *15* years (fold); in *25* years. b)　Draw yourself (folding the paper as before): as you see yourself; as you think your parents see you; as you think your teachers see you.	Back into twos to draw themselves in other situations (see opposite), followed up by discussions in small groups. Open up the paper and compare your view of yourself now and in the future. Discuss with your partner. Follow-up questions might ascertain whether pupils are satisfied/dissatisfied with what they see; what they would like to change; and then, perhaps, one first small step *they* could make towards change.

NOTE: How do we surround ourselves with family, friends and acquaintances? How important are they to us? How close do we like them to come? How close do we allow them to come?

One helpful way of exploring our life-space is by means of a simple linear diagram in which we place ourselves – ME – in the centre.

Pupil Objectives	Activities	Organisation and Method

To look at the part he and his fellows play in groups in the classroom, out of school, and at home, and to develop some awareness of the different parts which people play in different situations, and of how easily people can become fixed in their roles.	*THE PEOPLE AROUND US*
	
	a) Pupils make a list of people who feature in their lives a great deal:
	
	e.g. mother)
	     father)
	     brothers) these may be
	     sisters) names or roles,
	     friends) as the pupil
	     teachers) wishes.
	     others)
	
	b) Each pupil then constructs a diagram showing how these people cluster round them on their lists – some nearby, some farther away, e.g.
		It is helpful if the teacher constructs a personal diagram (see illustration) on the board to demonstrate the idea, showing that it includes working relationships as well as family and friends. (Teacher colleagues may be a 'collective'.)
		
		It is easy to demonstrate by the length of line which connects ME to others whether the person drawing the diagram feels that a relationship is close or more distant.
		
		Pupils can be encouraged to work in pairs to help one another. Discussion with a partner helps to clarify relative distances.
		
		The teacher may encourage a general discussion in which individual pupils talk about their own diagrams (see opposite).
		
		The diagrams may be kept until a later occasion when the activity may be repeated and comparisons made.

To show concern and provide support for his peers, when statements about difficulties or anxieties are heard.	Friends at Friends at school (can Youth Club Mother be named or not, as ME Sister Father desired) Form teacher *Discussion* – What makes a person close: being a confidante? being needed? trust? reliability? Does everyone necessarily need people close around them? Do some people like more space?	*NOTE:* It is important that this activity is undertaken in a friendly, easy way, with no coercion to complete the list or include the names of friends, if pupils are reluctant. It should be pointed out, also, that diagrams may fluctuate daily or weekly, according to events and feelings, and that it would be interesting for pupils to keep their diagrams to compare with those which may be drawn at a later date.

Pupil Objectives	Activities	Organisation and Method
To examine his own behaviour in a variety of circumstances, especially those which may lead to conflict with adults.	*AUTHORITY* What is meant by authority? Do you think of authority as a person? Is it always someone with power – to stop you doing something? Can it be someone with knowledge, an expert – an authority on . . .? Are you an authority on something?	Class discussion on what the word 'authority' means. Pupils identify the people in school and at home who they feel have authority – trying to focus a) on people who hold positions of authority and b) on people who have an authoritative manner. The teacher organises the class into pairs and the pupils prepare dialogues which they might carry out with various authority figures. (See examples opposite.)
To look at the part which he and his fellows play in different situations, and consider how easily people can become fixed in their roles.	*Situations* Examples Enquiring about a train or bus time from an inspector or conductor. Asking a policeman the way. Returning an overdue library book, or a borrowed item to a friend. Asking an elderly person to repeat something because you did not hear or understand correctly. Complaining to a neighbour that his TV is too loud. Taking a message to the headteacher.	Pupils should be encouraged to consider whether they should employ a different approach, according to the authority figure involved, and to consider the kind of response they might get. Follow up by asking: Does a uniform make a difference?

Pupil Objectives	Activities	Organisation and Method
To examine his own behaviour in a variety of circumstances, especially those which may lead to conflict with adults.	*AUTHORITY* (continued) *Parents* When my father tells me what to do, I . . . . When my mother tells me, I . . . . When I come home late, they . . . . I like my parents when . . . . I become angry with my parents when	The teacher organises the class into fours, and suggests statements which the pupils complete verbally and discuss. The pupils may be encouraged to consider whether or not difficulties in communicating with parents and other adults may be partly a result of their own manner of approach. The way in which they are treated may be beyond their control, however, and this may be simply an opportunity to share grievances.
To look at the part which he and his fellows play in different situations, and consider how easily people can become fixed in their roles.	*The Generation Gap* Examples of situations which may be used to demonstrate differences in the way in which some older and younger people perceive things. How much pocket money should a 12 to 13 year-old receive? How late should a young person, say 12 to 15 years, be allowed to stay out? How much work should a young person be expected to do in the house?	In pairs, the pupils take turns in assuming the role of the older person in one of the examples opposite. They should decide first who or what kind of person they will be representing. Each example may be 'acted out' by two pupils in front of the class, followed by discussion, or the pairs may choose a situation for themselves and investigate it. The teacher will circulate and ask pairs to demonstrate, where a useful discussion point is being raised.

14

Pupil Objectives	Activities	Organisation and Method
To understand, through demonstration, how facts can become distorted when a story is told and re-told.	*WHISPERED RUMOURS* 1 A circle activity for any number of participants. 2 *Discussion* a) How much had the statement changed? b) When more than one statement is being passed at the same time, can the statements become confused? Do people mix up or confuse the 'stories' which they carry in this way?	1 Arrange the group in a circle. a) One person is selected to whisper a simple statement – e.g. 'How much is a sack of potatoes?' – to the person on his left, who in turn whispers what he has heard to the person on his left. This continues until the statement has been whispered round the circle. The last person then relates the statement which he has received to the rest of the group for comparison with the original statement. b) This activity can be repeated with two different statements being sent round the group simultaneously – one clockwise, the other anti-clockwise. In each case the statements are passed right round the group and the two last people repeat the statements which they have received, for comparison with the originals. 2 At the end of both a) and b) discussion follows. At some point one person will find himself being offered both of the statements at the same time.

Pupil Objectives	Activities	Organisation and Method
To understand, through demonstration, how facts can become distorted when a story is told and re-told.	*WHISPERED RUMOURS* (continued) 3 *Further Discussion* a) How does a story become distorted, even with best of intentions, when it is shortened for re-telling? b) I don't believe it! Have you found yourself saying this when someone insists that an unbelievable story about someone you know is *TRUE?* c) How easy is it for apocryphal stories to be born, perhaps unintentionally, by the linking of separate incidents into one story. d) Do you think that some people pass on such stories, even though they don't believe them, because they make a good story? e) Gossip! What is gossip? Do you think that gossip can begin in the ways in which we have seen here? Is it harmful?	3 Experience has shown that even the shortest and simplest statements can be distorted when passed round a large circle. Interesting extensions of these activities are: a) To lengthen the statement to 12 to 15 words or more, so that some paraphrasing becomes inevitable. b) When two statements are being circulated simultaneously, make them closely related (e.g. different yet similar incidents concerning different people). c) The class could even try to 'invent' some such apocryphal stories in groups and try them out on other groups.

AUTUMN TERM

Pupil Objectives	Activities	Organisation and Method
To demonstrate how different people interpret what they have seen.	*'DID YOU SEE WHAT I SAW?'*	**You will need:** Pencil or felt-tip pen, sketch pad, or paper
		Arrange the group in a circle. One person draws a stick picture illustrating a certain situation.
		This is shown to the person on his left and on his right.
		They make a silent interpretation of the picture and whisper their deduction to the person next to them. One interpretation goes clockwise and one goes anti-clockwise half way round the circle.
		The last two pupils in the half-circle repeat the stories which they have received. The group then compares them with each other and with the original interpretation, which in turn is compared with what the 'artist' had really meant to illustrate.
	Discussion a) Apparently, we may all witness the same incident yet 'see' different things. b) Why do we 'see' different things? Is it due to eyesight, concentration, or what we bring to the situation, e.g. – the kind of people we are; our past experience; our beliefs?	Discuss.

17

AUTUMN TERM

Pupil Objectives	Activities	Organisation and Method
To continue to develop listening skills and become aware of variation in ways of perceiving situations.	*SIX EARS LATER* *Points to Reinforce* We filter out things that are unimportant to us – aurally and visually, i.e. we do not always hear correctly; we perceive things differently. Guessing what a simple mime or role play represents could be a further example of perceptions influenced by our own experiences.	Ask six pupils to volunteer to go out of the room. The six outside may be given a picture to consider whilst they wait, being told that they may later be asked to describe this picture to another group of pupils. The remainder of the pupils study a picture together and decide how to describe it clearly and accurately. Bring one pupil into the room and show him the picture for two minutes. Then bring in pupil number two, and ask the first pupil to describe the picture to him. Pupil number three is then brought in, and pupil number two describes the picture, and so on. The class should keep very quiet and listen intently. After the sixth description, the picture is displayed. The class comments on the accuracy of the final description, and points out where and why mistakes were made. **You will need:** Two or three attractive and brightly coloured pictures, with some detail contained in them, e.g. a reproduction of a well-known painting.

18

Spring Term

NOTE: Work on Study Skills, Revision and Homework was begun in the First Year programme and was further developed in the Second Year. The Third Year work on Key Facts is a reminder of the need to consolidate and continue these processes.

Pupil Objectives	Activities	Organisation and Method
To know what is involved in independent study and revision, and to demonstrate that, through practice, the pupil is reinforcing his powers to scan, summarise, interpret, recapitulate, take notes and present work effectively.	*STUDY SKILLS KEY FACTS I*	A period spent in recalling the work done in the Second Year on picking out key facts: ringing, underlining, using key questions to elicit key facts and making 'Key' diagrams would be the best possible introduction to this work.
	Refer to previous work in First and Second Year.	Some of the Second Year exercises might be worth repeating. The relevant sections in the *Second Year Book* are: *Using Diagrams* p. 37 *Active Reading* pp. 48-49.
		You will need: APPENDIX 4: Sample for Key Facts, *Sunnyhurst Woods*, paper
	Read the passage individually.	Arrange the class in pairs, giving each pair the passage in APPENDIX 4 to read. It would be useful to identify key features in the passages beforehand, as a check list. Pupils are asked to read the passage individually and then, with a partner, to discuss and identify key features, to test their capability in listing key facts.
	Discuss and identify key features. List these in order, keeping each one brief.	
	Relate the passage to another pupil, using the key facts as a guide.	Now break the class into groups of two pairs. Give each pair a different passage to read through and discuss, as before. Next, ask each pair to write a key fact list for their passage. One of the pair then uses the list to retell the passage to a member of the other couple, who has not read the same passage.
		Encourage pupils to recognize the benefits of this technique.

SPRING TERM

Pupil Objectives	Activities	Organisation and Method
	Group discussion Was it easier to remember this way? How much information did you need, i.e. was just one word sufficient, or did you need more? The practice of summarising the content of a conversation, a talk, a lesson, a given passage, briefly and quickly, and relating it there and then to another person, who seeks to understand what is said and to clarify it, when necessary, by asking simply, 'Do you mean . . .?' has been found to provide positive reinforcement of what has been said, written, or learnt, and to be an active preparation for revision.	Further practice, using material from different departments, is essential if the pupils are to develop these skills and relate them to all their subject work. Follow up with a short period of discussion. The key facts lists should be kept for use later on.

SPRING TERM

NOTE: The idea for this game came from a U.N.E.S.C.O. associated schools and colleges project for international understanding.

Pupil Objectives	Activities	Organisation and Method
To develop the ability to discuss reasons for choices and practice and to develop communication skills by outlining arguments.	*WHAT TO THROW AWAY* The activity is designed to be a light-hearted decision making exercise. 1 The pupils decide which item they would throw out first, second, etc, and be ready to explain why they have placed the objects in that order. 2 'Is my list different from yours?' 3 'My decisions are the soundest.' *Agenda* I chose . . . because	You will need: APPENDIX 5: *What is Absolutely Necessary* 1 The teacher gives out copies of APPENDIX 5 and then explains that each pupil is in a hot air balloon which is descending rapidly. In an attempt to maintain height, items from the list have to be discarded, one by one. *N.B.* The pupils will no doubt press the teacher for further information, such as 'Where do we land?' 'Are we rescued?' It is important to resist these questions and give no information at all, so that the pupils have to find their own reasons on which to base decisions. 2 The pupils compare lists in pairs or small groups. The teacher may wish to compile a scale of preferences on the blackboard, showing which items appear most/least often, etc. 3 An extension of this activity is to have one or two people in each group trying to persuade the others to change their order of preference. Pupils should be encouraged to listen to the reasons given by the 'persuaders' in (3) and be willing to change their minds if the reasons seem logical, i.e. not to be stubborn or obstinate without good reason. After a few minutes, see how many people have been won over.

SPRING TERM

NOTE: This unit of work is designed to support and prepare the way for those colleagues who are concerned with subject choices at the end of the third year, and not to usurp their function. The purpose of the unit is to make the pupil aware of the reasons why subject options usually have to be made towards the end of the third year, in the belief that this will produce more aware and recipient participants in the option process.

Pupil Objectives	Activities	Organisation and Method
		This unit spreads over three full sessions, I, II and III.
To recognize the presence of choices in school, and to recognize the necessity for such choices and the difficulties associated with them.	*TWO INTO ONE WON'T GO!* *MAKING SUBJECT CHOICES I* 1 Which subjects have we studied so far? Will we do the same kind of work in the fourth and fifth years? How might it change? What other subjects/activities might be added in the fourth and fifth years?	You will need: APPENDIX 6: Card A and Action Research Cards for duplicating, cutting up and distribution 1 Arrange class into small (mixed ability) groups and give out Card A, which is to be used as an introductory activity.
To begin to assess the qualities and attainments which upper school work will demand.	2a *Action Research* *What do parents and friends think we should be doing in fourth and fifth year?* The first of a series of Action Research tasks designed to supply this information. *Blackboard summary*	Lead the discussion round to the need for more information (from other people) on which to base fuller and more informed discussion. You will need: Lined paper
To begin to identify influences from other sources which can be brought to bear on his educational decisions.	Items suggested by the class for inclusion under the heading: – 'When we leave school we think that our parents will expect us to be able to . . .' The class copies out the blackboard summary to take home with them as an agenda for Action Research with their parents. See Introductory Note on Action Research, p. xxi.	Ask the groups what they think other people expect of young people when they leave school. Compile a blackboard summary from their suggestions. Allow a certain amount of broad speculation and suggestion on this theme and then narrow the field down to the possible expectations of parents. Approaches to outside bodies should be role-played and rehearsed, beginning with a shared exercise about some of the necessary attainments for school-leavers.

Pupil Objectives	Activities	Organisation and Method
To begin to assess the qualities and attainments which upper school work will demand.	*TWO INTO ONE WON'T GO! MAKING SUBJECT CHOICES I* (continued) 2b *Role Play* Ask pupils to take this form home and ask their parents:	Give out lined paper and ask everyone to copy the list from the blackboard. At the bottom of this ask them to write: Further Suggestions.
To begin to identify influences from other sources which can be brought to bear on his educational decisions.	i) Is this what you think I ought to be doing in the upper school? ii) Should I be doing all or only some of this? (Put ticks or crosses on the summary.) iii) Are there other things which you think I ought to be doing/studying in the fourth and fifth years? (Add these under Further suggestions.) Follow up with role play preparation (see 2b opposite).	2b After introduction (2a-b), ask one group to *role-play* one of their number approaching his parents with his enquiry form. Possible approach: Who is going to be Dad/Mum? Who is going to present the questionnaire? When will you do it? Before tea? After tea? What will you say? Why are we doing this? Now let's try it out .... (Get class to offer criticisms, suggestions, help.)
	2 Pupils discuss with their partners whom they are going to approach with this card. When they've agreed with each other that these are good choices, they write the chosen names on the card, as a reminder.	You will need: APPENDIX 6: Copies of Action Research Card 1 Arrange pupils in pairs within their groups. Give out Action Research Card 1 – one each. Ask them if they understand what the card is asking them to do. Check this by doing the exercise opposite. It might be suggested to the pupils that the people whom they approach might write a short answer on the back of the card.

SPRING TERM

Pupil Objectives	Activities	Organisation and Method
To recognize the presence of choices in school, and to recognize the necessity for such choices and the difficulties associated with them. To begin to assess the qualities and attainments which upper school work will demand. To begin to identify influences from other sources which can be brought to bear on his educational decisions.	*MAKING SUBJECT CHOICES II* 3 *Reporting Back* *'This is what our parents expect'* Prepare a blackboard summary from the Action Research findings. Then add to this 'Our older friends suggest . . .'. The findings from further Action Research will be listed under this heading later. 4 *Action Research* (continued) *What do other people think we should be doing in the fourth and fifth years?* Preparing to approach sixth-form tutors, employers and others, using Action Research Cards 2, 3 and 4 (APPENDIX 6).	3 *One Week Later* a) Arrange the class in groups, as before, and ask them to prepare a report on what they have discovered. b) Ask them who is to present their report. Encourage the rest of the group to support the presenter. c) From the report back, list on the blackboard (or overhead transparency*) the suggestions for fourth and fifth year work from parents and older friends. (Retain this list for the next session.). *If an overhead transparency is prepared (using felt-tips) instead of a blackboard summary, it can be retained for use in the next session. 4 Ask the members of the class to turn round with the minimum of movement to form groups of three. You will need: APPENDIX 6: Several copies of Cards 2, 3 and 4, cut up for distribution. Then hand out one copy of each of Cards 2, 3 and 4 for each group to consider. Ask them to read the cards and discuss them together to make sure they understand what each card is asking. Ask whatever supplementary questions are necessary to ensure this. E.g. (Card 2): What is the sixth form? (sixth form college) How old are pupils in the sixth form? What are they preparing for? What exams are they taking?

24

Pupil Objectives	Activities	Organisation and Method
To begin to assess the qualities and attainments which upper school work will demand.	5 *What we want to know* A short list should be drawn up from the class's offerings, which might include headings such as: What qualifications, if any, are needed for entry to the firm? What subjects might be important later? What ought we to know when we leave school?	5 Now work through Action Research Card 3, quickly, with the whole class, until you have completed a blackboard list of about six or seven local firms which are to be approached. Then work through 'What do we want to know?/What do we want to find out from these firms?' by question, answer, prodding (see opposite). When this list is drawn up, break the class up into seven or eight groups, according to their choice as far as possible:
To begin to identify influences from other sources which can be brought to bear on his educational decisions.	Then, the following items could be added: Do you see life in the upper school as as being all about: (i) exams (ii) job-finding? If not, what else do you think it should be about?	one group to approach one firm each; one group to approach sixth-form tutors.
	6 *How do we approach the firms/tutors?* By letter: What goes into it? What are we asking for? How do we set it out? Who writes it? By meetings/interviews: Who'll represent the group? What will he say/do? How does he greet people? How does he leave people? Will he/she need an agenda to help his enquiries? What should go into this agenda?	6 *Role Play* Pupils in their small groups work through the agenda opposite with guidance, prompting and small bouts of role play initiated by the teacher. Work through this sequence, making decisions about the content and carrying-out of letter-writing and/or interview. Finally – give out copies of Action Research Card 4 and ask each pupil to do as much as possible on this exercise before next week.

SPRING TERM

Pupil Objectives	Activities	Organisation and Method
To begin to assess the qualities and attainments which upper school work will demand.	6 *How do we approach the firms/ tutors?* (continued) Card 4 seeks to involve all pupils with the minimum of fuss, so that everything is not left to the various group representatives who carry out interviews.	6 *Role Play* (continued) You will need: APPENDIX 6: Copies of Action Research Card 4 There is a great deal of work in this unit, and it is unlikely that there will be time to lay much emphasis on this part of the exercise.
To begin to identify influences from other sources which can be brought to bear on his educational decisions.		

Pupil Objectives	Activities	Organisation and Method
To begin to assess the qualities and attainments which upper school work will demand.	MAKING SUBJECT CHOICES III 7 Reporting Back This is what society appears to expect . . . Add to the blackboard summary from the previous session, the latest Action Research findings, in order to highlight the need for (informed) advice.	7 One Week Later i) Arrange class in groups, as before, and ask them to prepare a report on what they have discovered in response to Action Research Cards 2, 3 and 4. You will need: Overhead transparency, if one was made in the previous week.
To begin to identify influences from other sources which can be brought to bear on his educational decisions.		ii) Ask them to decide who is to present their report. iii) As the report back proceeds, list on the blackboard all the subject demands and other expectations which local society seems to have of its schools and school-leavers.
To recognize the presence of choices in school, and to recognize the necessity for such choices and the difficulties associated with them.	8 Opting Getting Two Into One! This activity helps the pupils themselves to realise the wide range of choices and possibilities, and to realise also the impossibility of doing everything, of meeting all demands, resulting in the need for choice and a different form of organisation in the upper school.	8 You will almost certainly produce a list which is far too long and too comprehensive for any pupil to tackle (hence the title of the unit). Proceed by asking the groups to consider and discuss within and between groups questions such as: How long is your week? How many periods do you have? If you divide the number of subjects on the board into your number of periods for the week, how long do you get for each? Is it enough? How can we get more time for some subjects? (Do they all need the same time? Do we drop some subjects?)

SPRING TERM

Pupil Objectives	Activities	Organisation and Method
To begin to identify influences from other sources which can be brought to bear on his educational decisions. To recognize the presence of choices in school, and to recognize the necessity for such choices and the difficulties associated with them.	9 *Giving Advice* Drawing some conclusions from the evidence accumulated and from the ensuing discussions. The different groups could be asked to report to the rest of the class the kind of advice that they would give. 10 *Is It All Work and No Play?* You could go on for ever, but time is limited, so round off quickly with a short burst of lively discussion on a) and b)opposite.	If you had to drop any subjects, which would you drop? (Remember what sixth-form tutors, employers and more experienced people have said.) 9 Now ask each group to give advice to a person, about the course of study he should follow in the fourth and fifth years in order to: become a joiner/electrician become a lawyer/banker work in a shop/factory become a clerk/secretary become a teacher become a journalist/broadcaster join the Forces run his own business become a draughtsman/architect/designer/commercial artist One person from each group could play the role of a school-leaver wishing to enter a particular line of work and the rest of the group could offer advice. 10 Class discussion: a) Are the courses which you've just recommended concerned only with exams and getting jobs? b) Should there be another side to these courses concerned with: leisure recreation hobbies/interests knowing more about your world and about people?

SPRING TERM

Pupil Objectives	Activities	Organisation and Method
To be able to consider attitudes: giving up too easily, being influenced by others, going along with the rest, etc.	11 *Problems! Problems!* I've made a mistake, sir! Can I change from Physics to Art? Class discussion along the lines suggested opposite, so that the pupils may appreciate for themselves that the making of choices can both *open* and *close* doors to opportunities in later life. Items related to this section can always be returned to again for a few minutes from time to time as the need arises.	11 What happens if someone gets the wrong advice, or makes a mistake in their choices? Can they change their options? What will be the difficulties about changing? Can they catch up? Will it mean hard work? Why do people change? Will a change necessarily be for the better? (Out of the frying pan . . .) Is there a time when changing subjects becomes very difficult/impossible? If you make a mistake, or you change as a person, can it be remedied at a later stage in your education? Reference might be made to the findings of Action Research Card 4, to see how many people change direction over the years.

NOTE: Several activities are offered. Time may preclude completion of all of them, and so a choice made on the teacher's preference, with his particular tutor group in mind, is suggested.

Pupil Objectives	Activities	Organisation and Method
To recognize the presence of choice in school as an introduction to the presence of choices in life; to recognize the necessity for such choices and the difficulties associated with them.	*CHOICES I* 1 *TV Viewing* APPENDIX 7 contains a list of programmes for one evening's viewing on TV. APPENDIX 8 is provided for the pupils to indicate their choices for that evening's viewing. The incomplete sentences are intended to help them to realise that choices/decisions are involved. 2 *Role-play the following situation:* You are on holiday together as a group, and have one TV in your lounge to share. It has rained hard all day, you are beginning to get on each other's nerves, and you have to decide what you are going to do that evening. The programme choice is the same as in APPENDIX 7, which you have already completed.	You will need: APPENDIX 7: *TV Viewing* APPENDIX 8: *My Choice of TV Programmes* 1 a) Distribute APPENDIX 7 and APPENDIX 8. b) Explain that this activity is the first part of a three-part activity, and that the success of the whole activity depends upon pupils carrying out the first part properly. c) Whilst APPENDIX 7 is being completed, the teacher may choose to leave his pupils to fill it in unaided, or offer help to certain pupils. This stage is intended to be an individual exercise. Group discussion comes in the next part. d) Organise the class into groups of five or six. Groups might be formed to encourage as great a clash of tastes as possible. This can be arranged by studying completed Part 1 papers. 2 Use the same groups as in 1d above. Ask one group to role-play the situation in 2 opposite. Discuss the role-played situation in groups and then follow up with discussion of what you are going to do in the evening, and make out a time-table.

Pupil Objectives	Activities	Organisation and Method
To identify the influence which friends can have upon decisions.	3 *Agenda For Discussion* a) Did you agree with each other in your choice? Why, or why not? b) Was the eventual choice of TV programmes satisfactory for you? If so, why? (Was it because you got your own way, or for other reasons?) If not, why not? c) What were the difficulties you faced? d) Write down why you, as an individual, chose to follow the time-table you have written down. e) Do you think it is easier for a group or an individual to make choices on such a matter as TV programmes? Why? f) Are you often in this situation in real life? g) Do you think you should make your choices for subjects to be studied in school in the same way? Why, or why not?	Whole class discussion led by the teacher with the class still arranged in small groups, using the suggested questions as an agenda. (See notes on step-by-step discussion on p. xvi.) Emphasise that the discussion in Part 3 should endeavour to be as objective as possible, rising above the petty disputes or arguments of Part 2. You will need: Rough paper

SPRING TERM

Pupil Objectives	Activities	Organisation and Method
To recognize the presence of choice in school as an introduction to the presence of choices in life; to recognize the necessity for such choices and the difficulties associated with them. To identify the influence which friends can have upon decisions.	CHOICES II *Decisions! Decisions!* 1 Read through and answer APPENDIX 9. 2 Discussion in small groups of the following: a) Make a list of the events in life, over which a person has little or no influence or choice. An obvious beginning is a person's own name. Would you have liked to have a choice with your own name? Add more examples to this list. b) Do you always want to have a choice, e.g. would you like to be able to choose the sex of a child you and your partner may have when you marry? Make a list of any circumstances you can think of where you would not like a choice. c) Can you think of any situations that have occurred in your life already, or are likely to do so in the future, in which you will not be able to choose what you like? Why?	You will need: APPENDIX 9: *Decisions! Decisions!* Rough paper 1 Distribute sheets and amplify or explain where necessary. The questions at the bottom of the sheet can be answered on the reverse side, or on a sheet of rough paper. 2 Form small groups. The teacher may wish to change the formation of the groups from those in *Choices I* and yet again for *Choices III*.

32

SPRING TERM

NOTE: After many activities introducing the idea of choice and the necessity for it at some stage, pupils must make specific choices from the subjects offered by their own particular school. Whether tutors wish to begin work on CHOICES with the specific activities below, rather than the other more general activities, will be a matter for personal preference and consideration of the particular school's own system.

Pupil Objectives	Activities	Organisation and Method
To assess himself accurately; understand the others' assessment of him; make choices of subjects and levels that reflect his abilities and aspirations most appropriately.	**CHOICES III** 1 *Time is Precious* Complete APPENDIX 10 and, if pupils have different colours for different subject exercise books, then invite them to complete the table in the appropriate colour. 2 *Let's Be Frank* After the teacher's introduction to this activity (see next column), the pupil fills in APPENDIX 11, after guidance from the teacher, following up with the graph work if desired.	You will need: APPENDIX 10: *Time Is Precious* Coloured pencils, if required 1 The point to be made by the teacher is that the reason for making a choice is concerned with time, i.e. the more deeply you study any subject, the more time you need for it. Beyond the third year, there isn't enough time for everybody to study everything. Distribute APPENDIX 10, and assist where and when appropriate. After completion, some discussion should take place between neighbours or nearby groups or those who have completed the sheet quickly. The tutor may wish to arrange deliberately which persons should discuss together. When appropriate, move on to activity 2. You will need: APPENDIX 11: *Let's Be Frank* Graph paper or drawing paper and rough paper, coloured pencils, if required. 2 The teacher should make two basic points which the pupil has to weigh up, a) and b) below. The first activity has indicated what the school thinks is important in terms of the subjects studied in the first three years, and the time allocated to them.

Pupil Objectives	Activities	Organisation and Method
	3 *Agenda for Discussion* Look at graphs (or points) for Ability. a) Which kinds of subjects get most points? Are they similar in any way? b) Which kinds of subjects get least points? Are they similar in any way? c) What makes you good at a subject? Look at your graphs (or points) on Likes and Dislikes. a) Make out a list of what makes a subject interesting or boring. b) Which kind of subjects do you seem to like/dislike? Do these seem to be the same as those you are good at/not so good at? c) If you had done a similar exercise last year, would the points you have awarded each subject have turned out differently? d) Have you increased your interest in some subjects, or decreased in some? e) Why has this happened?	Now it is the turn of the pupil. The pupil is to consider: a) which subjects he/she is good at; b) which subjects he/she likes. Assist pupils in completion of APPENDIX 11. Depending on individual circumstances, the graph work may be omitted or added to, at the teacher's discretion. 3 *Small Group Discussion* The teacher may wish to conduct this activity with speed, giving a limited amount of time to discuss each individual question (see agenda opposite), so as to focus the pupils' attention on the question in hand, or prepare questions on the blackboard or paper for groups to discuss at their leisure, as they complete the appendices. *Follow-Up* If the teacher wishes, the pupils could be asked to take their work home to discuss with parents, and a useful follow-up tutorial discussing the graphs and the parents' responses could be held. In addition, personal discussion with pupils on an individual basis may be fruitful as the time for making options draws near.

SPRING TERM

Pupil Objectives	Activities	Organisation and Method
	4 Compare your lists or graphs with the graph for the time spent on subjects (i.e. APPENDIX 10). Do you like or dislike the subjects you spend most time on? Why? Are you successful or unsuccessful in the subjects you spend most time on? Why? Are you good at the subjects you like? Why? What have you learned about yourself in carrying out all these different exercises? Will the exercises help you when it comes to choosing your options? In what way?	4 Still in small groups, carry out the comparisons and discuss the findings (see 4 opposite). Move round the groups picking up points which are worth relaying to the other groups for their consideration. (See note on step-by-step discussion, p. xvi.)

Pupil Objectives	Activities	Organisation and Method
To know what is involved in independent study and revision, and to demonstrate that, through practice, he is reinforcing his powers to scan, memorise, interpret, recapitulate, take notes and present work effectively.	*STUDY SKILLS* *KEY FACTS II* a) Using the key facts sheet from the last study session (see page 19 – Key Facts I) to relate the contents of the passage as fully as possible. Did it work? Did the key facts list re-act on memory? If not, what would? b) Can fuller passages be constructed from a key facts list? c) *Perceptions* Did you recognize what was important?	You will need: a) Key Facts Sheet produced from APPENDIX 4 b) A prepared list of key facts relating to a topic of your choice a) The pupils should use their key facts sheets from the previous study skills activity and relate what they remember about the original passage to a partner, who may have the passage to refer to. This activity is intended to refresh the pupils' memories on the key facts method, and should take five to ten minutes. The pupils then compare notes about personal methods of remembering things. b) The teacher prepares and distributes a key facts list which the pupils have not previously seen. Working in pairs, they re-construct a passage from the brief details they are given. c) In pairs, one pupil relates a personal story as fully as possible, e.g. something that has happened recently – what he/she did yesterday, at the weekend, etc. The other notes down the words or phrases which he/she recognizes as key facts. They compare notes and discuss the importance or relevance of the facts noted.

NOTE: This unit can be used at any point considered appropriate. After a series of units on choices, a complete change of emphasis may be desirable, which is why this unit is included here.

Pupil Objectives	Activities	Organisation and Method
To continue to develop listening skills, and become aware of variation in ways of perceiving situations.	*RUMOURS* a) Perceptions again – the teacher may refer back to the activity of describing a picture, used in *Six Ears Later* p. 8. Can we distinguish facts from our own interpretation? What does 'keeping an open mind' really mean? b) Have we been victims of rumours or misinterpretation? How did it arise? What were the consequences? Do we *listen* enough?	a) A picture with a more social content may be shown after asking six pupils to volunteer to leave the room. They are the 'outsiders'. A pupil who has seen the picture describes its contents and what is happening, to 'outsider' number one, who then describes the information received to outsider number two, and so on. The teacher and the rest of the class may make a note of pupils' personal embellishments, and confront them with them afterwards. b) Ask the pupils to find three or five others to work with. Pose the questions opposite. It may be that the consequences were merely a feeling of being misunderstood, which might influence how we behave in a similar situation in future.

SPRING TERM

NOTE: It may be preferable to tackle this activity out of sequence, when a specific incident involving the school is reported in a newspaper, in order that it may be seen to have greater relevance to the lives of the pupils.

Pupil Objectives	Activities	Organisation and Method

To develop the ability to select issues of social/topical relevance from the media; to be able to discuss them critically with a small group of his peers, and to practise and develop his communication skills by interpreting and summarising an argument in the report back to other groups.	*CRITICAL FACULTIES I*
	
	Do the Papers Tell The Truth?
	Use a local newspaper to compare the newspaper report and an eye-witness (what really happened) account of a recent local incident.
		You will need:
		Copies of recent local newpapers
		Sheets of writing paper
		
		1 Obtain copies of local newspapers which have reports of either:
		
		  a) some information or incident involving the school; or, if one is not available at the time of this activity,
		
		  b) some account of a happening locally, of which some members of the class have first-hand knowledge.
		
		2 Split the class into small groups.
		
		3 Read the account to the class and ask for comment where necessary.
		
		4 Ask the pupils to discuss the account against the background of the comments made by classmates in the whole-class session, and also against the background of their personal knowledge.
		
		5 Groups report their findings back to the whole class, and the teacher lists inaccuracies, exaggerations and omissions on the blackboard.
		
		6 Each group is now asked to draft its own 'revised' version of this incident, and appoint a 'scribe', who will draw upon the collective ideas of his group in writing this revised version.

	An extension of these activities might be to invite pupils to treat in a similar way, some topic of which they themselves have a particular first-hand knowledge.	

Pupil Objectives	Activities	Organisation and Method
	An alternative might be to reverse the roles and have the different groups construct 'press' type accounts of these incidents, later comparing where each group laid emphasis and why.	7 One person from each group will read out his group's account of the incident, and the class will choose one of these accounts, which might then be pasted alongside the original newpaper article on the class notice-board. 8 In the ensuing discussion, ask the class to consider the difference between their version and the newspaper version of this incident. If it is marked, how misleading, or inaccurate, might accounts be in national daily newspapers.

Pupil Objectives	Activities	Organisation and Method
To develop the ability to select issues of social/topical relevance from the media; to be able to discuss them critically with a small group of his peers, and to practise and develop his communication skills by interpreting and summarising an argument in the report back to other groups.	*CRITICAL FACULTIES II* *It's Difficult to be Fair* or *Is It Difficult to be Fair?* 1 Discussion in small groups on the fairness or otherwise of the reporting of an issue of topical interest, with particular reference to the stand-point of the writer. 2 Whole class follow-up discussion: Is there concensus? What is fairness? 3 Concluding discussion in new small groups. What did we overlook before?	You will need: Sheets of writing paper 1 a) As and when social/topical issues with a particular interest for the form group are reported by the media, organise the form into small groups of approximately five or six. Try to include in each group elements for and against the issue(s) concerned. b) Each group discusses the issue and each group member writes his own brief summary for the others in the group to read. c) Discussion follows, focusing on differences which might still exist between accounts, despite the attempts to be as fair as possible. 2 Call the whole class together to draw out the general conclusions from each group. Ask the class to consider: is there any concensus of opinion? if not, what stands in the way of this? is fairness only as fair as the person writing the report? 3 a) Re-divide class into new small groups which contain one member from each of the previous groups. b) Exchange the ideas which their previous groups discussed and list any points their previous groups might have missed.

SPRING TERM

NOTE: *FRIENDSHIP* This item can stand alone as a unit on TRUST.
It also serves as a useful introductory activity to the next unit FRIENDSHIP.

Pupil Objectives	Activities	Organisation and Method
To be able to develop further the confidence to speak in the company of others by recounting personal experiences to the tutor group. To show concern and provide support for his peers when statements about difficulties or anxieties are heard. To show sensitivity to other people's feelings, for example, by being able to take on their 'role' or to describe how it feels to be a person in a given situation, or to infer a person's point of view or feelings from what is seen as his behaviour. To create a caring atmosphere in the group.	*CAN I TRUST YOU?* *CAN YOU TRUST ME?* *Note:* Trust is an abstract concept. It can be discussed; but without some real experience of what it is to trust someone, the concept will not be really understood. (Please read introductory notes on Practical Trust Activities, p. xxv.) *Agenda For Discussion* Allow the pupils to exchange feelings about the activity as freely as they are able; then focus on: Which did you like best, leading or being led? Did you feel safe? Did you depend solely on your partner, or did you use your own hands to guide you? Did you find it difficult to keep your eyes closed? Did you hear better? Could you keep track of where you were?	The pupils are asked to find a partner, either a friend or anyone they wish to choose. One of the pair will be 'blind', the other leading him around the room, making him feel 'safe' and at the same time describing colours, textures and the arrangement of furniture and position of other people. It is important for the teacher to encourage the pupils in a quiet and authoritative way, so that they cease to be embarrassed or silly and begin to feel that they are safe or unsafe, according to how their partner is leading them. After some time, the partners should exchange roles, so that each has a turn at both leading and depending on someone else. If it is possible, it makes the experience more worth while if the pupils can go out of the room and into more unfamiliar surroundings. Alternatively, the activity could take place in the school hall or gym, to provide a more challenging situation. If the pupils have quietened down and are treating the activity seriously, valuable discussion may take place afterwards about how they felt. If there has been too much noise and silliness, it is better to stop and say, 'We will try this again another time when we feel less embarrassed.' In any case, it is useful to return to this activity several times to help to build up feelings of trust in the group, encouraging the pupils to try different partners each time.

Pupil Objectives	Activities	Organisation and Method
To be involved in his own personal growth through an examination of his self-picture, feelings of self-esteem, and the way others see him. To be able to develop further the confidence to speak in the company of others, by recounting personal experiences to the tutor group.	*FRIENDSHIP* (See note at top of p.41.) Note: It is useful to precede discussion about important topics like friendship, with trust-building exercises, which help the pupils to focus on what they really feel, rather than on what they think they ought to be saying. 	The teacher asks the pupils to find another person to work with, perhaps the same partner as in the previous 'blind trust' activity. It is helpful if the teacher constructs a personal friendship pattern[1] on the board, during the discussion about what a friend is. (One line in each circle indicates one friend or acquaintance.) Example: A close friend: perhaps someone whom we know very, very well, and who knows us and accepts us as we are. Other friend: someone we like a lot and who seems to like us, but is not quite so close. Acquaintances: People we acknowledge and greet, but would not miss if we did not often see them. [1] This 'Life Space' approach to friendship is described in more detail in Dr. L. Button: *Friendship Patterns of Older Adolescents* (unpublished paper), Swansea University.

SPRING TERM

Pupil Objectives	Activities	Organisation and Method
	Agenda For Discussion How many *close* friends can you manage? What would happen to your friendships if you moved away? Where and when do you see your friends? Is it important how often you see them? How long does it take to make a close friend? Is there a difference in friendship within the same sex and between the sexes? How do you break off a friendship? What would cause you to want to break it? *What Are We Like With Our Friends?* Thinking of situations which arise with our friends, and how we respond and behave.	If the pairs of pupils are able to discuss these questions freely with each other for a few minutes before the teacher suggests the next point on which to focus, all will have an opportunity to explore their own attitudes to friendship. They will *all* have an opportunity to express their thoughts, rather than waiting for a turn to speak, some never being brave enough to speak up, as would happen in a whole-class discussion. The teacher will be circulating, encouraging the less articulate with extra comments or questions and, if a useful point has been made, asking the others to pause for a moment to hear it and consider it themselves. Two pairs of pupils join together to form a group of four and think of a friendship situation, either real or imaginary: e.g. breaking off a boy/girl friendship; being let down; trying to make a new friend. Each four prepares a short role play of such a situation to present to the others (see introductory notes on Role Play). Discussion about each situation would follow; e.g. how it arose; how the people behaved; what was missing; causes and effects.

SPRING TERM

Pupil Objectives	Activities	Organisation and Method
	Focusing On Making Friends How much opportunity do we have to make new friends? Do we wait for it to happen, or do we help to make it happen? *THE FRIENDSHIP GAME* (APPENDIX 12) a) Which of the boys and girls represented on the cards are most likely to be friends? b) Who do you think might find it most difficult to make friends? c) Who would you choose to be your friend? d) What about boy/girl friendships? Are there any boys and girls who you think might get on well together? e) Who would you not like to know? A final question could be: 'How would you describe yourself?' This could be a written description, if time allows, which could be kept to refer to at a later date.	You will need: APPENDIX 12: *The Friendship Game* Still in fours, the teacher gives out the descriptions of people, as in APPENDIX 12. The groups are asked to consider the cards and agree on their response to the questions in the agenda opposite.

SPRING TERM

NOTE: *HEALTH AND SEX EDUCATION.* Much work in health and sex education may already be covered in other subject areas, and the form teacher may decide accordingly whether or not to omit these activities from tutorial time. It has been assumed that teachers will be aware of their own Authority's policy on who deals with sex education and what may be taught.

Pupil Objectives	Activities	Organisation and Method
To understand the physical changes which take place during adolescence and relate them to the personal growth and development of himself and his peers. To be involved in his own personal growth through an examination of his self-picture, feelings of self-esteem, and the ways others see him.	*THE TEENAGER'S BODILY NEEDS* The questionnaire, APPENDIX 13, can be completed (boxes marked 1) and discussed, but scoring the answers can be deferred until the questionnaire has been completed a second time (boxes marked 2) at a later date, when the two sets of scores are compared and differences discussed. *A Year Older* Refer back to the activity in the second year, *'WHAT DO I LOOK LIKE?'* and consider how opinions might have changed since then. Points for discussion: How did the boys regard the girls in the second year, and vice versa? Have opinions changed now that pupils are in the third year? Are differences more pronounced?	You will need: APPENDIX 13: *The Teenager's Bodily Needs* The pupils complete the questionnaire, APPENDIX 13, individually. The teacher explains that these will be collected and kept for a few weeks so that they can be completed again, to see whether there are any changes. Items on the questionnaire can be discussed with the full group, e.g. 'How many put a) for question 1?' Or the pupils can be asked to get into groups of four and discuss any of the items which interest them. In fours, the pupils consider the differences between one another, e.g. height, weight, size of feet, especially the differences in height, weight, size of hands, feet, between the sexes. This discussion is in preparation for a film on adolescence. Pupils should be encouraged to express any embarrassment they may feel and then consider the subject in a sensible manner.

SPRING TERM

Pupil Objectives	Activities	Organisation and Method
	If it can be obtained, the film *AND THEN ONE YEAR* is a useful lead for a discussion on adolescent development.	You will need: Film *AND THEN ONE YEAR* available through the Authority's Health Education Officer
	Check-List of Terms Used in the Film: adolescence, acne, erection, menstruation, puberty, pubic hair, pituitary gland, sex hormones, testicles, sperm, ovary, womb (uterus), wet dream.	In small groups, preferably fours, the pupils discuss the film and the terms which they have heard and may not fully understand.
	Why are we embarrassed to talk about some of these terms openly?	If the pupils do not mention some of the terms, it may be because of embarrassment, and the teacher may wish to help the pupils to consider their own feelings.
To show sensitivity to other people's feelings.	*Problem Page* Some people have no one whom they feel they can talk to or ask questions, and so they turn to complete strangers and write to magazines.	Who can they talk to or ask, when they want to know something? *NOTE*: If a film of the teacher's own choosing is used, the check-list in the activities column will need to be amended.
	Agenda For Discussion What are the problems which appear most often? What do you think of the advice given?	The teacher may provide examples, or ask the pupils to bring examples, of problem pages in teenage magazines. These are read, in small groups, and discussed. Pupils, in pairs, are asked to consider what questions or problems they would like to raise. These are written down anonymously and redistributed for suggestions and advice. The teacher may wish to 'vet' the problem letters before distributing them.

SPRING TERM

Pupil Objectives	Activities	Organisation and Method
To show concern and provide support for his peers, when statements about difficulties or anxieties are heard. To examine his own behaviour in a variety of circumstances, especially those which may lead to conflict with adults (e.g. parents and personal appearance), and be able to see his own behaviour from the other's point of view.	*Adolescent Behaviour* Some teenagers refuse to change for games/P.E., or to take a shower with the rest. Others, girls especially, find themselves blushing often, or feeling near to tears. Why is this? How can strong feelings be coped with? If a person is shy, moody, bad-tempered, etc., how do the rest of us respond? How do you respond when your parents say you look a mess?	In fours, the pupils discuss a situation which has occurred recently, either in school or to an individual in the group. This could be role-played, to show us what happened, who was involved, what was said.

SPRING TERM

NOTE: This activity applies the idea of receiving and entertaining a visitor to discover some specific information from a visiting expert, in this case a Health Visitor.

Pupil Objectives	Activities	Organisation and Method
To be able to add to his competence in social skills and to his ability to plan agendas and carry through conversations with adults.	*FINDING OUT FROM THE EXPERT* If several queries have arisen during the previous activities and the pupils show a genuine wish to find out more information, the teacher may suggest inviting a Health Visitor to the tutor group. The visitor should be well primed also that it is not a 'lecture' situation, but a conversation in which knowledge and information are asked for and given.	The teacher asks a group, say six or eight pupils, to prepare to receive the visitor; practising the arrangements for meeting him/her, the introductions, seating arrangements, what we want to know, etc. (See Introductory Note on *Using Visitors*, p. xviii.) This group may conduct the visit on behalf of the class, who simply listen in, or they may have given in a question which is asked on their behalf. If there is sufficient interest, the whole form could take part in the conversation with the visitor.

Summer Term

Pupil Objectives	Activities	Organisation and Method
To be able to explore his corporate ownership and responsibility for community property, and to identify ways in which this responsibility may be exercised.	*THE A – Z GAME* Who are the people we take for granted? Do we know someone who fills these tasks? How well do we know them? Did they plan to have that job, e.g. a teacher, a caretaker, a doctor?	You will need: APPENDIX 14 a: *The A – Z Game* A *blank* set of answer boxes APPENDIX 14 b Answers to *The A – Z Game* The pupils could complete this game, APPENDIX 14 a, in twos, as a competition. Although this is a light-hearted look at other people's jobs, it could be used as a starter for a deeper consideration of other people's work in the local community and of how much we take for granted.

Pupil Objectives	Activities	Organisation and Method
To identify the specialist opportunities and facilities which exist locally for leisure. To locate and identify clubs/groups outside school, in which people can participate.	*WHERE I LIVE AND THE PEOPLE I MEET* *Agenda* I live at . . . . The street where I live is . . . . I go to a club . . . . The nearest shops are . . . . The launderette is at . . . . The nearest church is . . . . The doctor is . . . . The nearest hospital is at . . . . My friends live in . . . . The library/museum is . . . . It opens at . . . . For leisure activities . . . . *Suggestions For Research* Where do parents go for an evening out? Where do grandparents go? What do parents with young children do about babysitters? How do old people get about? What is public transport like?	You will need: Large sheets of paper, felt pens In pairs, or groups of four, the pupils are asked to consider the neighbourhood where they live. The agenda opposite may help to focus on less obvious points. If time allows, pupils from the same street or area could compile a sketch map of their area, showing shops, library, clubs, pubs, etc. If not much is known about facilities in the area, pupils could be encouraged to find out more about it, and add to their maps during the next tutor period.

SUMMER TERM

Pupil Objectives	Activities	Organisation and Method
To co-operate with his tutor group in identifying the kind of positive short-term contribution which can be made to the local community.	*WHAT IS A COMMUNITY?* Sometimes people in a community have a difficult time because of the environment, e.g. heavy traffic, type of housing, etc. For example, the local community is not such a good place for me because . . . The local community is not such a good place for . . . (old people, teenagers, mothers with young children) because . . .	Arrange the class into small groups. Ask each group to decide what they mean by the word 'community'. Share these interpretations with the rest of the class. Encourage pupils, in groups, to consider what makes their community a *good* place to live in. They could then think of things which make it not such a good place (as opposite).

To explore his corporate ownership of and responsibility for community property, and identify ways in which this responsibility may be exercised.	*Can Anything Be Done?*
	Who should put these things right?
	
	a) A busy road with no pedestrian crossings
	
	b) Highrise flats where the lifts never work
	
	c) Nowhere for children to play
	
	d) An old person who is cold and lonely
	
	Think of a problem which could be dealt with by:
	
	    a neighbour
	    a policeman
	    a tenants' association
	    a friend
	    this tutor group
		The teacher asks the pupils, as a class, to think about the bad things.
		
		Is anything being done about them?
		
		Can anything be done?
		
		Whose responsibility is it?
		
		Is it always the council's responsibility?
		
		Can people look after each other and do something to improve things for themselves?

Pupil Objectives	Activities	Organisation and Method
	Can Schools Do Anything? Does this school have something called Community Service?	You will need: Local newspapers
	If so, who takes part, what do they do? Do they enjoy it?	The teacher encourages the pupils to find the answers to these questions themselves.
		If Community Service is carried out by older pupils, perhaps a group of these could be invited to tell the class, also in groups, what they do.
To explore the idea of corporate ownership of and responsibility for community property, and identify ways in which this responsibility may be exercised.	Local papers may be a source for finding out what is being done, and what could be done. E.g. headlines such as: VANDALISM CLOSES TODDLERS' PLAYGROUND	Alternatively, the teacher in charge of community work could be invited to discuss what the pupils have discovered for themselves, things which they feel need to be done, and which they could tackle.

SUMMER TERM

Pupil Objectives	Activities	Organisation and Method
To explore corporate ownership of and responsibility for community property, and identify ways in which responsibility may be exercised.	*TRAFFIC LIGHTS* An activity for six players, about the immediate environment, i.e. the street/road where we live. With less able pupils, some discussion of the street cards may be necessary, e.g. to identify which are safety items, etc. *Rules* 1 Each player chooses a street number (numbered 1 to 6 on the board) and places his coloured counter on it. He chooses a name for his street and writes it on his score sheet. 2 The street cards are shuffled, and each player picks six cards from the pack, which is placed face down on the table. The player can look at his cards and lay them out in front of him. The remaining cards are placed in a pile, with the top card face up beside this pile. 3 The player who is on Street 1 begins the game by throwing the dice and moving in a clockwise direction, starting from the green light. Each player then takes his turn.	In moving round the board the player is seeking to collect the Street Cards which will enable him to develop his street in the way in which he would like it to be developed. You will need: 1 Street Sheet per group (enlarged 4 times) (APPENDIX 15a) 1 set of Street Cards (APPENDIX 15b) 2 sets of Change Cards (APPENDIX 15c) 6 coloured counters to play with 1 score sheet for each street (plain paper) 1 dice and shaker, or spinner The activity is carried out in groups of six. With smaller groups, some pupils could 'develop' two streets. Each player develops his own street: alternatively, each group could work corporately to produce the best group of streets in competition with the other groups. The end result should be a street (or group of streets) which has a good balance of amenities. Every street *must* include housing, shopping facilities and at least one safety factor (see the rules opposite).

SUMMER TERM

Pupil Objectives	Activities	Organisation and Method
To explore corporate ownership of and responsibility for community property, and identify ways in which responsibility may be exercised.	*TRAFFIC LIGHTS* (continued) *Rules* 4 The players move twice round the board to complete the game. 5 Landing on red means that no card can be taken and exchanged. Landing on amber means that only the card which is face up beside the pack can be taken and exchanged. The player does not have to keep the card which he has just picked up but he must place one card, face up, on the discard pile. Landing on green, the player takes two cards to exchange. These may be either two (unseen) cards from the pack or the card which is face up and one from the pack. He does not have to keep the cards which he picks up, but he must put two cards face up on the discard pile. 6 If a six is thrown, move the counter six places and make an exchange as required. The player then either takes another throw or exchanges another card. 7 If a player is in the street next to his own, the second time round the board, he may choose to miss one or two turns if his street has not been 'developed' to his satisfaction,	Initially, it may be helpful to play the game with only one group participating, in order to demonstrate the rules and procedures to the rest of the class. *Exchanging Cards* When a player draws a Street Card he may *exchange* it for a card which he already holds or he may reject it.

54

Pupil Objectives	Activities	Organisation and Method
To explore corporate ownership of and responsibility for community property, and identify ways in which responsibility may be exercised.	*TRAFFIC LIGHTS* (continued) *Rules* exchanging one of his cards each time, instead. He must move at the third turn. He should remember that another player may get 'home' before him whilst he remains stationary. 8 When the first person is back after moving *twice* round the board, play stops and each player lays his Street Cards in front of him and tries to arrange them so that his street is developed advantageously. 9 Scores for the street are worked out with the help of a partner. (See Scoring Scale (APPENDIX 15 b)). If a street does not contain housing, shopping facilities, or a safety factor, the player does not score. Each player has the value of his street scored by a partner.	Pupils are encouraged to discuss the scores to be given for each of the cards in each player's street. Housing scores up to 10, but the player and his partner must discuss the value of the housing on his particular street, e.g. if a player has only 'a large empty house' in his street, he must make a good case for how it could be used to provide housing. Shopping, similarly, scores up to 10 marks. A safety factor scores 5 and, again, the players must agree on what is a safety factor, e.g. the pupils may not realise that pavements are a safety factor in the street. Up to 25 additional points may be scored after discussion of the player's hand, if the player's partner agrees that the ways in which the player has chosen and combined his cards provides additional bonuses, e.g. a pleasant environment, full/varied employment, opportunities for a wide range of recreation. Up to 5 marks can be given for any of the other Street Cards.

SUMMER TERM

Pupil Objectives	Activities	Organisation and Method
To develop an appreciation of environmental factors which determine the quality of people's lives, by learning about influences which may be beyond one person's control.	*TRAFFIC LIGHTS – DEVELOPMENTS* Change cards can be introduced as a development of the activity, when pupils are used to the first stage. *Procedure* N.B. Players should retain the cards with which they finished the first stage. They move round the board once more picking up Change cards – two when they stop on green and one when they stop on amber. The players keep the cards until the end of the game. They then put one Change Card next to an appropriate Street Card, and add or deduct the points shown on the Change Card from their original street score. If they have two or more change cards which are appropriate to one street, they may choose the best one.	This stage of the activity may need more explanation, especially as the use of the Change cards differs from the use of the Street Cards. After the first player arrives 'home', play stops and the players lay out their Street Cards and their Change Cards, and discuss whether their street has been improved by the changes which have been made.

SUMMER TERM

Pupil Objectives	Activities	Organisation and Method
To develop a recognition of his own responsibility for and contribution to the community to which he belongs.	*TRAFFIC LIGHTS – FOLLOW-UP* a) What would an 'ideal' street look like?	The groups are asked to use the pack of Street Cards to lay out an ideal street. Each group can then decide the criteria by which they have made their choices, i.e. *why* they have chosen the particular combinations.
To develop the ability to put forward a rationale for his ideas and be able to see himself in relation to what is happening around him.	b) Draw up a rating scale.	A master list of all the items used then can be drawn up together with a rating scale, as suggested by the groups: e.g. 4 for pavements 5 for street lighting and so on. Minus marks may be used for some items, e.g. derelict houses.
To develop a growing awareness of political influences which operate in his own environment.	c) Rate your own street. d) Questions: What do you think is missing from your street? What don't you like in your street? Who has paid for what is in your street? Have the people who live there any say in what their street is like?	The pupils may use the scale to rate the street or community in which they live, subtracting marks if an item is present in the street but not in good repair, e.g. broken paving-stones, street lights out. Follow-up discussion based on an agenda similar to that given opposite (d).

57

SUMMER TERM

Pupil Objectives	Activities	Organisation and Method
To be able to review his progress to date realistically, both from his own point of view and the point of view of others.	WHAT HAVE I ACHIEVED THIS YEAR? 1 *Academically* Consider whether personal objectives, previously stated, have been achieved.	You will need: APPENDIX 16: *What Have I Achieved?* *Personal Review Sheet*
To discuss, with the teacher, his own feelings about his progress at different stages in the year; to identify those things he would like to alter or develop, and determine the steps by which this can be brought about.	APPENDIX 16 provides a series of questions which can be posed as an individual written exercise. Discussion in small groups beforehand could be useful preparation with pupils who have difficulty with writing; or, where time is limited, the questions could be used as an agenda for small group discussion.	The pupils may be reminded of the *Know Your Own Skills* exercise which they completed in the Autumn Term, and consider how far they have achieved their personal goals.

To have the opportunity of discussing his own attitudes to school work and how they affect his progress and achievement, e.g. giving up too easily, couldn't care less, going along with the rest.	2 *Practically*
	    To consider how much responsibility has been undertaken during the year.
		Pupils, in pairs, consider what practical things they have undertaken, perhaps for the first time, during the year. Examples might be:
		
		    The weekly shopping
		    Cooking meals
		    A part-time job
		    Going camping with friends
		    Car maintenance
		    Helping someone on a regular basis

SUMMER TERM

Pupil Objectives	Activities	Organisation and Method
To extract the basic concepts of the year's tutorial programme, namely, personal responsibility for his own behaviour and learning.	**3 Personally** a) *The Computer Game* Considering how each person in the group has grown and developed.	You will need: APPENDIX 17: *Computer Game* This activity was used in the Autumn Term of the second year, and is re-introduced at this stage with a slightly different focus. The APPENDIX 17 provides questions which can be cut up and distributed singly to the pupils, who are arranged in circles of six or eight, with one volunteer in the centre of each circle. Go round the circle with each person in turn asking a question of the 'computer'. The middle person, the 'computer', turns to face someone who, in their opinion, best answers the question. The 'computer' should be changed several times, and the questions can be asked more than once, as each new 'computer' may give different answers.
To show concern and provide support for peers, and show sensitivity to other people's feelings.	b) *Being Constructive* An attempt to encourage the pupils to try genuinely to help one another. *N.B.* It is important to encourage support, i.e. not just criticism.	After the Computer Game, the pupils may be asked to pair off, or stay in groups, if they are working seriously, and consider the questions on APPENDIX 17 which refer to personal qualities, i.e. questions 4 and 5. The teacher could circulate, listening to the discussion and encouraging support, with occasional comments and questions, such as, 'What could so-and-so do then?'
To be involved in his own personal growth through an examination of his own self-picture, feelings of self-esteem, and the way others see him.		

SUMMER TERM

Pupil Objectives	Activities	Organisation and Method
To grasp and distil the essence of the third year, by suggesting ways in which the tutor group can help the next third year.	*MEMORIES OF THE YEAR* a) What things stand out?	The teacher could start by telling the group about his/her own outstanding memory of the year, either in school or outside, and then ask if someone else has a memory to share. This would be a short whole-class activity, followed by (b).

To extract the basic concepts from the year's programme, and to begin to recognize and accept responsibility for his own behaviour and learning.	b) What are our expectations?
	   In school?
	   Out of school?
	   What do we mean by expectations? Is it to look forward to or to dread?
		In small groups, discuss items from the following agenda, which are suggested gradually in step-by-step discussions.
		
		1 Will the fourth year be different?
		2 Will staff treat you differently, do you think?
		3 Will you work harder? Do more homework?
		4 Wear different uniform?

To be able to continue to recognize the qualities and attainments which upper school work will demand.		5 Will you take more responsibility in school? 6 Will you change friends because of different options? 7 Will you have a part-time job? 8 Will you expect to come in later at night? 9 Will you expect to do more or less at home? 10 Will you play games for the school? Hope to do well on Sports Day? 11 Will you join or continue in school societies, e.g. choir, drama group? 12 Will you do something new, take up a new hobby, or sport, e.g. tennis?

APPENDIX 1a:

KNOW YOUR OWN SKILLS — A GUIDE TO DECISION MAKING

Give yourself points out of five (e.g. 5 = very good; 4 = good; 3 = fair; 2 = weak; 1 = very weak).
Do it first in Column 1. Your friend will do it for you in Column 2. Then you will do it again later in
Column 3.

	Column 3	Column 2	Column 1
READING SKILLS			
1 Reading for pleasure			
2 Reading with understanding			
3 Reading aloud			
4 Reading quickly			
5 Remembering what you have read			
TOTAL POINTS GAINED			
WRITING SKILLS			
1 Writing for pleasure, e.g. letters			
2 Writing neatly			
3 Writing legibly			
4 Writing accurately, e.g. spelling			
5 Writing quickly			
6 Writing in note form			
TOTAL POINTS GAINED			
NUMBER SKILLS			
1 Using numbers for pleasure, e.g. puzzles			
2 Understanding charts and graphs			
3 Remembering tables			
4 Learning new mathematical processes			
5 Doing problems			
6 Measuring accurately			
TOTAL POINTS GAINED			
PRACTICAL SKILLS			
1 Making things for pleasure			
2 Using tools			
3 Planning a task			
4 Understanding how things work			
TOTAL POINTS GAINED			

	Column 3	Column 2	Column 1
ARTISTIC SKILLS			
1 Drawing for pleasure			
2 Drawing accurately			
3 Painting or colouring			
4 Designing			
5 Tracing			
6 Taking part in musical activities			
7 Listening to 'serious' music as well as 'pop' music			
TOTAL POINTS GAINED			
GENERAL SKILLS			
1 Asking questions in class			
2 Answering questions in class			
3 Working with a group of people			
4 Listening to the ideas of others			
5 Putting forward your own ideas			
6 Completing homework			
7 Revising for examinations			
8 Coping with examinations			
9 Concentrating on a given task			
10 Persevering until the task is complete			
11 Making up your own mind			
TOTAL POINTS GAINED			

APPENDIX 1b

KNOW YOUR OWN SKILLS – SUMMARY SHEET

Name of Subject you may be thinking of choosing as an option	Special skills needed in this subject (*Refer to the lists of skills in APPENDIX 3a*)	How many points have you scored in these skills?	Would this be a wise choice of subject? *Yes/No*

APPENDIX 2

PEOPLE WHO INFLUENCE US

	Grand-Parents	Mother	Father	Best Friend	Form Teacher	Brother	Sister		Other things e.g. TV, fashion, etc.
1 Choosing new clothes									
2 Choosing records									
3 Choosing where to go on holiday									
4 Choosing what to do on Saturday night									
5 Choosing a hairstyle									
6 Choosing what to do on Christmas Day									
7 Deciding whether to start your homework or go out									
8 Deciding whether to save or spend									
9 Deciding whether to take a part-time job									
10 Deciding whether to take an afternoon off school									
11 Deciding whether to finish with your boy/girl friend									
12									
13									
14									
15									

APPENDIX 3

WHY DO I LISTEN?

Why Do I Listen To My		Because That Person
Grandparents		Is willing to support me
		Wants me to succeed
Mother		Has the same likes as me
		Understands me
Father		Has time for me
		Expects me to fit in with their ideas
Best Friend		Knows how it feels
		Is concerned about me
Form Teacher		Is older than me
		Is responsible for me
Brother		Gives me no alternative
		Is experienced
Sister		Will listen to me
		Always tells me the truth
		Knows what I want
		Is someone I respect

APPENDIX 4

SAMPLE FOR KEY FACTS — SUNNYHURST WOOD

SUNNYHURST WOOD, the prettiest of all the beauty spots to be found for a great number of miles around Darwen, is the latest acquisition of the Corporation, and will permanently mark the Coronation of His Majesty, King Edward the Seventh. In looking about for a fitting permanent memorial, His Worship the Mayor (Alderman John Tomlinson) hit upon an appropriate and popular scheme in suggesting that the splendid glen at Sunnyhurst should pass into the possession of the town for preservation as a woodland park. The ambitious scheme was at once realised to be a very suitable one, and to Alderman Tomlinson future generations in Darwen owe a great debt of gratitude for the work he has done in carrying the scheme to a successful issue. Single handed, he tackled the various owners of the land at Sunnyhurst and, by persuasion, induced one and all to give up their property to the town without unreasonable charge. In this work he was absolutely untiring. He showed great enthusiasm and tact in the work to which he had applied his hand, and he earned the good will of all parties by the manner in which he dealt with their various interests. In addition, he personally solicited and obtained the greater part of the necessary cost, viz. £3,000.

Much has been done in the past to despoil the Wood, and rob it of many of its treasures, but the vandals' reign will now come to an end, and protection will be afforded, not only to the plants and trees, but also the many birds which frequent the Wood.

The principal walks which run in serpentine fashion through this place of beauty will be retained, but improved and properly drained for visitors and, with others intended to be added, their length will be about five or six miles. The total area is 85 acres.

From the new walk a panoramic view of the whole of the surrounding scenery can be obtained, as in the picture, which was specially photographed from the best situation on the site of the proposed walk, the terminus of which will be on the bank of the Earnsdale Reservoir.

Extract from the Souvenir Book
of King Edward VII,
dated June 26th 1902, describing
Sunnyhurst Woods at that time.

From Darwen Local History Collection.

APPENDIX 5

WHAT IS ABSOLUTELY NECESSARY

Put the articles in order of jettisoning.

Matches	
Blanket	
Maps	
Toothbrush and Towel	
Tools	
Cooking Utensils	
Pet Animal	
Torch	
Tape Recorder	
Compass	

APPENDIX 6

TWO INTO ONE WON'T GO

ACTION RESEARCH 1

From amongst your friends and relatives, talk to at least two people:

i) who left school a year ago;

ii) who are about 18-20 years old;

and ask them:

What subjects do you think we ought to study in the upper school?

What do you think we ought to know by the time we leave?

I'm going to ask:

Divide the back of the card into two answer spaces.

i) ....

ii) ....

ACTION RESEARCH 2

Find out from sixth-form tutors, either in school or at the sixth-form college:

i) What kind of courses are available in the sixth form?

ii) What do they lead to?

iii) What subjects do they include?

iv) What should we be doing in the fourth and fifth year to prepare for this?

Find out if they think that life and work in the upper school should be all about:

Examinations   Job finding

If not, what else do they think it should be about?

ACTION RESEARCH 3

Working with your teacher, choose a group of, say, six or seven local employers whose firms provide work in:

Electrical and/or general engineering

Local Government offices, banks, building societies, etc.

A factory

TO THE TEACHER

Add others relevant to your area to complete this card before it is handed out.

ACTION RESEARCH 4

Talk to as many adults as you can and ask them:

i) If they are still doing the kind of job they did when they left school.

ii) If they've changed the kind of job, e.g. from factory worker to dustman, or from clerk to teacher,

a) Have they changed more than once?

b) What made them want to change?

(Add other questions)

Write answers on the back.

CARD A

THIS IS YOUR SCHOOL.

In the first, second and third years you have studied:

English	History	Art	Domestic	Social and
French	Geography	Design	Science	environ-
German	Maths	Handicraft	R.E.	mental
Latin	Science	Needlework	P.E.	studies
			Games	

1 Do you think that you will go on studying these subjects in your fourth and fifth years?

2 Are there other subjects which should be added to broaden this list?

APPENDIX 7

TV VIEWING

	BBC 1		BBC 2		ITV
6-00 pm	Nationwide	6-00 pm	Open University	6-00 pm	Granada Reports
6-50 pm	Tom and Jerry	7-00 pm	Final overs in the Gillette Cup clash between Lancashire and Yorkshire	7-00 pm	Coronation Street
7-00 pm	Tomorrow's World			7-30 pm	The Big Film James Bond in *From Russia With Love*
7-25 pm	A Generation Game Special	7-30 pm	Showaddywaddy in Concert		
8-10 pm	It's A Knockout	8-00 pm	James Last's World of Music with guests	9-30 pm	George and Mildred
9-00 pm	News	9-00 pm	Pot Black Fred Davis and Alex Higgins	10-00 pm	News At Ten
9-25 pm	The Midweek Film *Carry On Sailor* with the usual *Carry On* team	9-30 pm	Mastermind Final	10-30 pm	The Spinners in Concert
10-50 pm	World Cup Football: highlights from today's preliminary round clash between Scotland and Italy	10-00 pm	Highlights of Tennis and Cricket: Tennis: Wimbledon Senior Finals Cricket: Lancashire v Yorkshire in the Gillette Cup	11-00 pm	Science fiction film *They Came From Beyond*
11-30 pm	Closedown	10-50 pm	Closedown	12-30 pm	Closedown

APPENDIX 8

MY CHOICE OF TV PROGRAMMES

TIME	PROGRAMME	CHANNEL	COMPLETE THE SENTENCES IN THE SPACE PROVIDED
6.00 pm	. . . .	. . . .	My favourite programme is (from the list in APPENDIX 6): . . . .
. . . .	. . . .	. . . .	My least favourite programme is (from the list in APPENDIX 6): . . . .
. . . .	. . . .	. . . .	. . . .
. . . .	. . . .	. . . .	I turned the television set off between: . . . . .
. . . .	. . . .	. . . .	. . . .
. . . .	. . . .	. . . .	My most difficult choice was: . . . .
. . . .	. . . .	. . . .	. . . .
. . . .	. . . .	. . . .	My easiest choice was: . . . .
. . . .	. . . .	. . . .	
. . . .	. . . .	. . . .	
. . . .	. . . .	. . . .	

APPENDIX 9

DECISIONS! DECISIONS!
LIFE AND CHOICE

Excerpts from the average life and the choices to be made.

1 Which rattle shall I play with?

2 Which primary school should I go to?
3 Which secondary school should I go to?

4 Which subjects should
I choose to study?

5 Which career or job do I want to follow?

6 Where do I want to work?

7 Whom shall I marry?

8 Where shall we live?

10 What names
shall we call them?

12 Shall I change my job?

9 How many children
shall we have?

11 How shall we bring up our children?

13 Shall we move house?

14 Shall I be buried or cremated?

Which period of your life seems to contain most choice? Why?
Which period of your life seems to contain least choice? Why?

Which do you think will be the hardest choices?
Which do you think will be the easiest choices?
Why should there be choice in life, whether we like it or not?

APPENDIX 10

TIME IS PRECIOUS

On this side of the chart, write down a list of subjects you are studying now. Fill in each column as indicated. What must you do to obtain your final total in Column 4?

SUBJECT	Number of periods per week	Length of periods (minutes)	Total time (minutes)

On this side of the chart, mark off the total minutes you spend on each subject in the appropriate square, and then shade the squares. When you have finished, discuss these points with someone else:

i) Why do some subjects have a lot of time and others only a little?

ii) If you could change the amount of time you spend on subjects, in what way would you do it? Which subjects would you spend more time on, and on which subjects less?

0	40	80	120	160	200	240	280	320	360	400

APPENDIX 11

LET'S BE FRANK

Write down the subjects you study in each column in the same order, as started off for you below. Then give yourself the points from 1 – 5, according to these guide lines:

1 = a subject at which you are very good
2 = a subject at which you are good
3 = a subject at which you are average
4 = a subject at which you are not good
5 = a subject at which you are very weak

SUBJECT – Measuring your ABILITY	Points 1 – 5
1 English	
2 Mathematics	
3	
4	
5	
6	
7	
8	
9	
10	
11	

1 = a subject which is one of your favourites
2 = a subject which you like
3 = a subject which you don't mind
4 = a subject you don't care for
5 = a subject you dislike

SUBJECT – Measuring your LIKES AND DISLIKES	Points 1 – 5
1 English	
2 Mathematics	
3	
4	
5	
6	
7	
8	
9	
10	
11	

GRAPH WORK Now, on a piece of graph paper or drawing paper, you are going to construct a graph which should help you to compare your likes and dislikes with your abilities.

On your paper, draw a long base line (x axis), and on the upright (y axis) mark a scale of 1 cm to 1 point. Then draw simple bars for each subject, putting likes and dislikes next to ability. Shade each subject a different colour, and add dots to that bar which shows likes and dislikes.

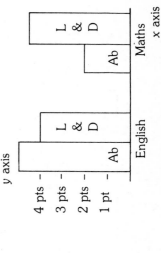

73

APPENDIX 12

THE FRIENDSHIP GAME

1 *My name is Julie.* I live near the school and have two older brothers who are now working. I like P.E. and games, and often play for the school netball team. I would like to teach P.E., but don't know if I shall pass all the exams I need.	2 *I'm Janet.* I've got two younger sisters and a lot of pets. My favourite pet is my dog, a red setter. I'm not very keen on P.E., and often bring a note to get excused, because I get lots of colds. I like watching telly, and usually stay in most nights.
3 *I'm called Freda.* I like watching football, and usually go to the home matches on a Saturday. I hate school and want to leave as soon as I can. I would like to work in a factory, because you can earn a lot of money. I go out most nights to a disco or to the youth club.	4 *Hello! My name is Anne.* I've got lots of brothers and sisters, and we have plenty of fun. I would like to be a nurse when I leave school. I often go to help at the old people's home on a Saturday. I go to the youth club and sometimes go to see a film or to the disco.
5 *My name is Hilary.* I have no brothers or sisters. I live with my parents, and I have a pony. I enjoy riding and would like to own a riding school one day. I like reading and listening to records.	6 *My name is Mahmood.* I was born in Pakistan and live here with my parents and three brothers. I like playing cricket and sometimes go to the swimming baths. On Saturdays I help my father in our shop. I would like to work in a garage.
7 *Hello! My name is Shaun.* I have two older sisters and a little brother. I like P.E. best, and play football for the school team. My favourite TV programme is the late night horror film. I support our town football team and like wearing the scarf wherever I go.	8 *I'm Daryl.* I like school and came top in English and History in the last exams. I would like to be a doctor or a vet. I don't like P.E. very much as I am not very good at games. I am learning to play a trumpet and, when I get better at it, will join the school band.
9 *I'm Robert.* I enjoy collecting things. I have 40 record sleeves and over a hundred different match-boxes. I like school as we have lots of fun, but I'm not very good at lessons or sport. I have a younger sister, and she likes to go with me to the skate-board park.	10 *My name is David.* I have some pigeons and I am teaching them to home, so that I can enter them in races. My dad often helps me to look after them. I'm keen on all sports, particularly cross-country. Last week I was the first in our group. I would like to work as an engineer one day.

APPENDIX 13

THE TEENAGER'S BODILY NEEDS or HOW WELL DO YOU LOOK AFTER YOUR BODY?

Put your answer in the box.

1 How often do you wash your face?

    a)   When you get up?
    b)   When you get up and when you go to bed?
    c)   More often?

2 How often do you take a bath or shower, or have a thorough wash all over?

    a)   Daily?
    b)   More than once a week?
    c)   Weekly?
    d)   Less than once a week?

3 How often do you put on clean underwear?

    a)   Every day?
    b)   Twice a week?
    c)   Not more than once a week?

4 How often do you put on a clean shirt/blouse?

    a)   Every day?
    b)   Twice a week?
    c)   Not more than once a week?

5 How often do you wash your hair?

    a)   Once a week?
    b)   Twice a week?
    c)   More often?

6 If you have a spot or blackhead, do you

    a)   wash your skin carefully but thoroughly?
    b)   squeeze the spot?
    c)   do nothing?

7 Girls, do you remove make-up before going to bed?

    a)   Always?
    b)   Usually?
    c)   Rarely?

8   Do you go to bed late

    a)   every night?
    b)   at weekends and during the holidays?
    c)   occasionally?

9   Do you take part in sport/games/P.E. and other exercise?

    a)   Regularly?
    b)   Never?
    c)   Occasionally?

10   Do you enjoy eating

    a)   chips with everything?
    b)   plenty of sweets and cakes?
    c)   plenty of fresh fruit and vegetables?

11   Are you happy with the way you look?

    a)   Yes
    b)   No
    c)   Not bothered

APPENDIX 13

ANSWERS

SCORES

1a – 1	1b – 2	1c – 3
2a – 3	2b – 2	2c – 1
3a – 3	3b – 2	3c – 1
4a – 3	4b – 2	4c – 1
5a – 1	5b – 2	5c – 3
6a – 3	6b – 2	6c – 1
7a – 3	7b – 2	7c – 1
8a – 1	8b – 2	8c – 3
9a – 3	9b – 2	9c – 1
10a – 1	10b – 2	10c – 3
11a – 3	11b – 2	11c – 1

If you have scored less than 15, you need take yourself in hand. Your body is suffering.

16 – 22   You are not giving yourself the treatment you deserve.

23 – 29   Quite good. You have learned how to look after your body.

30 – 33   Congratulations! You are the proud owner of a really healthy body.

APPENDIX 14a

THE A – Z GAME

The answer to each clue starts with a different letter of the alphabet.

1   His speed may save your life.
2   Just the person for building a good home.
3   He's on the staff of school, but never gives you homework.
4   He will help you get better.
5   He's sometimes called Sparks, but won't give you a shock.
6   He will cool down a hot situation.
7   His high speed pipes don't carry water.
8   Gives you style on top.
9   He welcomes the weary traveller.
10 Twelve of them have to decide guilty or not guilty.
11 Only men can have this job.
12 Persuading those in Clue No. 10 is their chosen profession.
13 A pint bottle he brings, foul weather or fine.
14 You rely on them to help you get better.
15 Bureaucracy's horrors he tries to put down – a go-between man for sorting out bureaucratic mistakes.
16 Their parties aren't fun, but they need your support.
17 Only women can have this job.
18 The town would be a mess without him.
19 A uniform they wear, but there is danger too.
20 They go to your school and you see them all day.
21 Everybody needs him in the end.
22 The same as Clue No. 4, but for animals, not for you.
23 When his job is done, you can see right through it.
24 We can't think of anything, can you?
25 At the club, he's there to help.
26 He looks after animals – but with a letter like Z, what else could he do?

APPENDIX 14b

THE A – Z GAME – ANSWERS

A	M	B	U	L	A	N	C	E	M	A	N
B	R	I	C	K	L	A	Y	E	R		
C	A	R	E	T	A	K	E	R			
D	O	C	T	O	R						
E	L	E	C	T	R	I	C	I	A	N	
F	I	R	E	M	A	N					
G	A	S	M	A	N						
H	A	I	R	D	R	E	S	S	E	R	
I	N	N	K	E	E	P	E	R			
J	U	R	O	R							
K	I	N	G								
L	A	W	Y	E	R						
M	I	L	K	M	A	N					
N	U	R	S	E							
O	M	B	U	D	S	M	A	N			
P	O	L	I	T	I	C	I	A	N		
Q	U	E	E	N							
R	O	A	D	S	W	E	E	P	E	R	
S	O	L	D	I	E	R					
T	E	A	C	H	E	R					
U	N	D	E	R	T	A	K	E	R		
V	E	T									
W	I	N	D	O	W	C	L	E	A	N	E	R
X											
Y	O	U	T	H	L	E	A	D	E	R	
Z	O	O	K	E	E	P	E	R			

APPENDIX 15a *TRAFFIC LIGHTS*

This plan should be enlarged four times for play.

Pedestrian Crossing.
Go forward
two places.

	Red	Amber	Green
Street 6			

School Crossing
Patrol. Go back
3 places.

Stop

Children Crossing.

TRAFFIC LIGHTS

| Red | Amber | Green | | Street 5 | Accident | Black | Spot | Red | Amber | Green |

Street 1

Green

Amber

Red

TRAFFIC LIGHTS

	Just man-aged to cat-ch it. Move on three.	No bus for one hour. Miss one turn.	Just missed it. Wait for next throw.
	Bus		Stop
Street 2	Green	Amber	Red

Accident
go back
3 places

Stuck in a
traffic jam.
Miss one
turn.

Road clear.
Move on
one place.

TRAFFIC LIGHTS

Green

Amber

Red

TRAFFIC LIGHTS

Street 4

Green

Amber

Red

Play Street. Go
forward one place.

Play Street
8 am
To Sunset

Street 3

Red Amber Green

Road Works.
Detour back
to Street 4 Amber.

APPENDIX 15b

STREET CARDS

Make a pack of cards, carrying the following items (with the number of copies indicated) — sixty cards in all.

HOUSING	*SHOPPING FACILITIES*	*SAFETY FACTORS*
3 of each	*2 of each*	*2 of each*
row of new detached houses	street market	traffic lights
two rows of older terraced houses	supermarket	pedestrian crossing
a large empty house	row of small shops	street lights
semi-detached private houses	post office	pavements
council houses	garage	
block of high-rise flats	chip shop	
one row of derelict terrace houses		

EXTRAS

disused cinema	Chinese restaurant	Branch library
mosque	bus shelter	public house
car park	church	trees
public convenience	clinic	telephone kiosk
flower beds	children's playground	bingo hall
park	coffee bar	a primary school
	small shoe factory	

SCORING SCALE — MARKS OUT OF 50
Housing scores up to 10 marks.
Shopping scores up to 10 marks.
A safety factor scores up to 5 marks.

25 MORE POINTS MAY BE SCORED
Recreational facilities. Employment opportunity.
Pleasant environmental factor. Facilities for
different members of the community.

*Partner may award up
to 5 marks for each
of these facilities.*

81

APPENDIX 15c

CHANGE CARDS

More people in the area. Shops increase trade. + 5	All catering establishments built up custom. + 5	Health Officer closes down catering establishment. – 5	Private houses lose their value. – 5
Private houses gain in value. + 5	Council houses in need of repair. – 5	Council houses sold to private owners. + 5	Sports Council grant for recreational facilities. + 5
Cut-back in grants restrict recreational facilities. – 5	Houses improved. + 5	Houses damaged by floods. – 5	Police suggest improvements to safety factor. + 5
Grants to all public buildings. + 5	Extra rates on public buildings. – 5	Houses come down to make way for new road. – 5	Extensions built on houses. + 5
Expanding Church increases congregation. + 5	Church closes lack of support. – 5	Place of employment gets export order. + 5	Environmental factor improved. + 5
Environmental factor damaged by vandals. – 5	Shop closes down from supermarket competition. – 5	Place of employment goes on short time. – 5	Safety factor damaged. – 5

APPENDIX 16

WHAT HAVE I ACHIEVED? PERSONAL REVIEW SHEET

1   In what ways has the third year been different from the first two years?

2   Are you satisfied with your options? Has your work during the second half of the year justified the choices you made?

Write a list of your options for the Head of Year, explaining why you chose each subject and what you hope to achieve in each one. Justify your choice.

3   What are your strong points at the end of this year? Are they different? Are they reflected in your choices?

4   You have obviously matured physically during the year. Have you matured as a person? Are you more grown up in

a)   your home life in your contribution to home and responsibilities?

b)   your friendships and attitudes towards others?

5   What has been your contribution to the group during the year? Have you helped or hindered the progress of others? In what ways?

APPENDIX 17

COMPUTER GAME – SUGGESTED CARDS

1 Who would you choose to look after your young brothers and sisters?

2 Who has grown most?   2a) Who has grown up?

3 Who has most overcome their shyness?

4 Who has overcome a difficulty?

5 Who is less troublesome than they used to be?

6 Who has helped you most?

7 Who has done most for the tutor group?

8 Who listens to you the most carefully?

9 Who would you ask to help you if you had lost your coat?

10 Who would you ask to help you if you were feeling ill?

11 Who would you ask to help you if someone were picking on you?

12 Who would you ask to help you if your friend had fallen out with you?

13 Who would you ask to help you if you had forgotten some important equipment?

14 Who is less noisy than they were?

15 Who have you got to know better this year?

16 Who is the most cheerful?

17 Who is the kindest?

18 Who would you choose to care for a stray animal?

19 Who would be the most willing to help an old person?

20 Who would be the most willing to welcome a newcomer?

21 Who has changed the most?

22 Who do you know least well?

23 Whose appearance do you admire?

YOU MAY FIND THE FOLLOWING TITLES USEFUL FOR SUPPLEMENTARY READING

L. Button: *Discovery and Experience*, O.U.P., 1971

L. Button: *Developmental Group Work with Adolescents*, Hodder & Stoughton, 1974

D. Hamblin: *The Teacher and Pastoral Care*, Basil Blackwell, 1978

Schools Council Project: *Health Education 5 – 13, Think Well*, Nelson, 1977

Health Education Council Project 12-18: *Living Well*, Cambridge University Press, 1977

D. Hamblin: Study Skills, Basil Blackwell, 1981

M. Marland: *Pastoral Care*, Heineman, 1974

K. Blackburn: *The Tutor*, Heineman, 1975